QUICK SINGLES

MEMORIES OF SUMMER DAYS & CRICKET HEROES

EDITED BY

CHRISTOPHER MARTIN-JENKINS
& MIKE SEABROOK

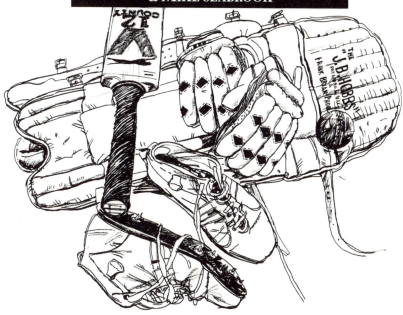

J M DENT & SONS LTD
LONDON · MELBOURNE

First published in Great Britain 1986

Copyright © Lennard Books 1986

British Library Cataloguing in Publication Data
Quick singles
1. Cricket
2. Martin-Jenkins, Christopher
796.35'8'0922 GV919

ISBN 0 460 04721 3

Made by Lennard Books
for J.M. Dent & Sons Ltd
33 Welbeck Street, London W1M 8LX

Editor Michael Leitch
Designed by David Pocknell's Company Ltd
Production Reynolds Clark Associates Ltd

Printed and bound in Spain by
Tonsa, San Sebastian

CONTENTS

INTRODUCTION
CHRISTOPHER MARTIN-JENKINS

*H*e still finds cricket – especially the actual playing of the game – the best way of fortifying himself now that he is the wrong side of forty. The number of cricket books he has written or edited is rapidly catching up the number of centuries he has scored. He'll have to give up soon, but not just yet.

There can be nothing in sport, and very little in life itself, to compare with that rare feeling of unalloyed joy, that awareness of good fortune mixed with sheer pride of self-achievement, which fills the heart and mind to bursting when having played a major innings, and won the match for your side, you make your way, red-faced and smiling, through a ring of cheering spectators, with your vanquished opponents treading wearily behind, themselves applauding.

It is not given to many, of course, to experience this in a Test match at Lord's. But to anyone who plays cricket in however humble a sphere and with however little skill, a variation on that moment of triumph always comes. For some it may be only a vital catch, perhaps fortuitously held; or the two wickets in an over which suddenly transforms a lost cause. But the moment will come and although its instant pleasure will fade, it will lie in the mind for years after, like a contented cat before the fire. For even the donkeys of cricket have their day as a hero:

Fools for I also had my hour,
One far, fierce hour and sweet,
There was a shout about my ears
And palms before my feet!

Any personal reminiscences in this anthology are of a modest, often self-deprecatory nature. Not everyone who has contributed was a cricketing donkey, by any means, but none was asked to write because of his aptitude for cricket – not even Peter Gibbs of Derbyshire or Lord Dunglass (as he then was) of Middlesex. What they have in common is an affection for the game and a feel for its romance. You may feel, as I do, that

4

there has been all too little old-fashioned Newboltian romance in first-class cricket as it has been 'sold' to the public, especially but not only in Australia, in recent years. The point is well made by Lord Home himself; also by Sir Robert Mark, Donald Steel and Paul Jennings, whose 'Quick Singles' all in different ways point out some of what has been lost.

Nostalgia, as our former Prime Minister warns, is a dangerous drug, and a present Premier, Robert Hawke, reminds us that there are many good things about the modern game, amongst them, perhaps, television, which gives accessibility to the fleeting heroes of the game as never before.

There can be no doubt, however, that distance lends enchantment to cricketing heroes past and present, and even to our own youth. Our boyhood games were infused with hopes and dreams. Those stalwarts of the North Country, Brian Redhead and Colin Welland, recall some of the improvisations which were necessary for street cricket and Henry Graham remembers his passionate commitment:

At night in light snow
under sodium lighting
two intent figures
at the nets without nets
in the centre of the road.

There was a time when no boy, like it or not, could avoid some youthful contact with cricket if his education was in England. Lawrence Durrell and the Maharajah of Baroda, although both have spent most of their life away from England, point to the essential Englishness of the game. And Ian Wallace, though he was brought up south of the Border, recognizes the disadvantage of having parents from a part of Scotland where the cricketing traditions did not run deep.

In England in the 1980s there are children who never play a game of cricket at school. Some, no doubt, will be heartily glad that they do not have to; others will be missing a source of immense fun, and a genuine means of learning about life and developing the character. All will be poorer inheritors of a traditional bulwark of every Englishman's education.

Although America and Canada now beckon more appealingly than the old Mother Country, the cricketing islands of the West Indies have not made the same mistake.

But we should not despair, because you cannot have children without mothers and fathers and it is almost always the father who first ignites the spark of a lifetime's affection for cricket. Few are the cricketing parents who do not feel that their son has inherited some special talent for the game and they are prepared to make great sacrifices, mother driving miles and baking endless cakes, father sneaking off from work to suffer in silence on some windblown boundary whilst their son walks out to bat, steeling themselves to react with only slightly less emotion to the elation, or despair, which their child will be feeling hours, or moments, later.

John Ebdon writes movingly about his own father, whose dying thoughts were an amalgam of cricket and war. Anyone who experienced either of the World Wars seems to have associated cricket with the lost life of home:

I see them in foul dugouts, gnawed by rats
Dreaming of things they did with balls and bats.

Most of the contributors to this anthology were, happily, born too late to share, like Siegfried Sassoon, the horrors of the trenches; but rather more cricket was played during the second War and, in the years after it, there was a general glorying in the return to normality which has left its mark on all who experienced it. Edwin Brock vividly describes how Len Hutton's 364, an epic spread over days, not hours, became the outstanding memory of the year before the war.

This was still a time when heroes were like distant gods. Their private lives were their own and people went to cricket just to see them. Barry Norman knew that Don Bradman would not let him down when he queued at Lord's in the early morning with an anxious eye on the clouds. Roy Hattersley, on the other hand, saw the great anti-climax of his last Test innings and felt that his own hero, Len Hutton, would never have disappointed him like that. Leslie Thomas provides a delightful insight into the quirky deadpan humour of Sir Leonard, whose amanuensis Leslie briefly was, and Donald Steel conveys the chivalry and buccaneering charm of Bill Edrich and, expectedly, Denis Compton, the happy genius.

Bradman, Hutton, Compton, Edrich: all mainly batsmen. Two of the truisms of cricket are that bowlers win matches but that spectators go to watch batsmen. Robin Bailey strikes a blow for the 'workers' with his memories of Larwood and Voce, or rather of his boyhood impersonations of them, but no-one is mentioned more often in these particular despatches than P. B. H. May. By pure coincidence, three Carthusians, Frederic Raphael, James Prior and Ian Wallace have all made mention of the influence of the school and its cricket on their lives. The first two were contemporaries of the great May whom Raphael remembers hating flattery and eschewing arrogance, almost as if to prove that the more you experience the heady feeling I mentioned at the outset of this introduction, the less you appreciate it. Glory is felt in inverse proportion to the volume of glorious moments?

I hope I have pointed your way to some of the pleasures in store for you in this collection of essays. There are plenty of others: Baroda on the advantage of being a cricketing Prince in India; Lord Orr-Ewing on the game in Corfu; Jeffrey Archer on how a daydream became a sort of reality; Basil Boothroyd on the distinctly unhumorous reactions of the humorist Bernard Hollowood after a defeat in Holland; John Fowles on the pleasures of his own career (proving that not everyone in flannels is a fool); Tim Rice and Jeremy Kemp, playing cleverly, like good students of Shakespeare, with names; Sir Eldon Griffiths on cricket as a legitimate diplomatic tool; and Michael Leitch and Mike Seabrook, who have both had much to do with this book, recording two very different experiences of cricket in the West Country. Not least William Deedes, that distinguished Editor, arguing that cricket is best during the stolen hours which have been devoted to it, when, strictly, one should be somewhere else.

I know so well what he means. I am past forty now, and I was a weekend late in writing this short prologue; all because I could not resist playing cricket on a cold, grey May afternoon. For someone paid to write and speak about cricket, the stolen hours are the ones spent actually playing the game. And, though the heady moment of triumph seldom comes, they are the best.

BRADMAN

BARRY NORMAN

Former opener who now bats from memory. An off-spinner, he is mostly used tactically by the Lord's Taverners to boost the opposition's run rate when they don't look like giving his team a game. Greatest achievements: dismissed Colin Cowdrey and Mike Denness twice each. Denness caught and bowled both times. One year dismissed Cowdrey at Arundel on Sunday and Denness at Scarborough the following Saturday – two England captains in one week: not bad for a village off-spinner.

The sky was heavy and overcast, distinctly unpromising; clouds waddling about like so many distended bladders seeking a convenient place on which to release their contents. Now, on such a morning, I would wait till around ten and then phone whoever I was going to the cricket with and say: 'What do you think? Doesn't look too good, does it? Leave it till lunchtime, shall we – see if it clears up?'

But then, well then I was just fifteen and by half-past nine I was already outside Lord's because I knew that God wouldn't let it rain, not really rain, on a day like this. The very existence of a game as lovely as cricket was in itself positive proof of God's own existence and surely He couldn't let the weather ruin the occasion for his favourite son, puzzling though it was that God, whom I always imagined in an MCC tie and an England touring blazer, should have chosen an Australian as his favourite son...

August 25, 1948: the first day of Bradman's last match at Lord's and my first and only chance, in the age before TV, to set eyes on the world's greatest batsman. And there I was, clutching my satchel with the sandwiches and the Tizer, and there was my friend Farrant, similarly equipped.

'Hello, Farrant,' I said, greeting him warmly.

'Hello, Norman,' he said. In those days public schoolboys didn't have first names, or if they did it was extremely bad form to refer to the fact.

We scurried along to the back of the queue which stretched away from the Grace Gates and right round the corner and almost to the car park.

And this was not a Test match either – merely the Australians v the Gentlemen and the Australians weren't even fielding their strongest side: Morris and Toshack weren't playing, neither were Tallon and Bill Johnstone.

But it *was* Bradman's last match at Lord's.

And it began to rain.

Farrant and I had barely taken our places in the free seats beside the Tavern, square on to the wicket, when one of those waddling, distended bladders relieved itself all over St John's Wood. I couldn't believe it.

'Farrant,' I said, 'it *can't* rain – not today!' And Farrant agreed with me. Nevertheless it was certainly raining and it continued, nerve-wrackingly, to rain – not for very long, I suppose, though it seemed like hours – until at last the bladder gave a contented sigh, fastened its trouser buttons and hurried away. Whereupon the sun came out followed shortly afterwards by the umpires and, to our joy, the Gentlemen.

The Australians had won the toss and Bradman would bat today – though not immediately. First there appeared S.G. Barnes and W.A. Brown, themselves figures of wonder to me.

In those days all my heroes, except Compton and Edrich, belonged most firmly to the 1930s, probably because I had read about first-class cricket far more than I had watched it. It was the literature of the game that had hooked me long before I had seen it played. And in 1948 most of cricket's literature stopped at the beginning of the war.

Barnes, the post-war player, I knew about and grudgingly admired because he scored 234 against England on the 1946–47 tour Down Under. But it was Brown whom I watched with the greater awe as he made his way to the middle because he belonged to that Golden Age of the Thirties when all Test cricketers were ten feet tall and the sun shone every day.

(The first match I ever saw was also at Lord's in 1945: England v Australia in a Victory Test match. Cyril Washbrook made a century that day and Bill Edrich scored 73. But the man I remember most vividly was Hammond, greatest of all England's heroes of the Golden Age and a man I had scarcely believed existed outside the pages of a cricket book. He came to the wicket, burly and belligerent, a dark blue cap surmounting that pleasantly ugly, froglike face and made 83 in hardly any time at all. I never saw him bat again but on that day he made me realize for the first time what an awesome thing a cover drive could be.)

Now, though, as the Gentlemen took the field there was no Hammond among them, for he had gone into retirement, but still there was his near-contemporary, Brown, and with him the younger Barnes, both of whom had engaged with England's former champion in many a titanic struggle. Another time it would have been thrill enough simply to watch these two bat, but not today. As in turn they took guard and prepared to face the bowling, Farrant and I fervently wished them gone. They were merely curtain-raisers, the cricketing equivalent of a juggling act on a variety bill, charged with warming up the audience before the star appeared. We wanted them out, one of them anyway and it didn't matter which.

They didn't keep us waiting long. Barnes went first, caught by Wilf Wooller for 19 off the bowling of a promising young Cambridge undergraduate named Trevor Bailey. An innings of 19 is not usually memorable but this one was for the sheer ferocity of Barnes's square-cutting. I have never seen its like since. This was not what passes for square-cutting nowadays, with the bat striking behind the ball in what is more of a square drive. This was the real, classic thing, the bat coming down on top of the ball and smashing it to the boundary with a

speed to baffle the eye and a force to break any hand misguided enough to get in its way.

But soon – too soon I think now with hindsight – Wooller held the catch and Barnes put his square-cut away for use another day and made his exit. There was a pause and then everyone in the Members' Stand stood up and so did we all, all of us in that packed ground, clapping till our palms were stinging red and continuing to stand and clap as the object of this veneration hurried to the wicket, tugging by way of acknowledgment at the peak of that weird, squat cap the Australians wear and walking briskly as if embarrassed by so much attention.

My first reaction was one of mild disappointment: he was smaller than I had expected, chunky but not tall. Hammond had seemed of appropriately heroic stature (probably a bit on the fat side, if the truth were told), big and imposing. Bradman, by contrast, looked almost slight and as he took guard and glanced around the field it was difficult to believe that such a man of such a build could have averaged 99.96 in all Test matches.

But when he started to bat... ah, what a transformation – not so much a smallish man as a giant of limited growth. I wish I could remember a particular shot he played, something as indelible as Barnes's square-cut, but I cannot. All I remember is that he seemed to have every shot I had ever heard of and played them all without favouritism, like the

father of an enormous family who is equally fond of each of his children and takes care to neglect none of them.

How could you set a field – how could you even set about bowling – to a man like that?

He didn't appear to recognize yorkers; to him they were half-volleys. Bouncers were simply long-hops to be hooked away with a roll of the wrists to the boundary behind square leg. Pitch short and he was immediately on the back foot cracking the ball through mid-wicket or the covers; toss it up and he was already three paces down the wicket, calmly deciding which section of the crowd would have the privilege of collecting this one.

They say that Bradman hardly ever raised the ball above the ground. Well, I can vouch for that. Eight Gentlemen had a bowl at him that day and if he hit a six off any of them I have no recollection of it. What I have in my mind is this image of the ball scorching across the grass as it came every time off the middle of the bat and as it went every time just where the fielder wasn't.

They also say – or rather *Wisden* says – that Brown, who scored 120, 'showed even more freedom than Bradman'. I don't remember that; indeed I hardly remember Brown at all except as a necessary figure at the non-striker's end. Elegant, yes, I believe he was that – graceful, too, and immensely competent. But essentially he was a foil, Horatio to Bradman's Hamlet.

'There are more things in heaven and earth, Horatio, than are dreamt of in *your* philosophy' and, crack, there went another drive that only Bradman could have played.

From the start we knew – Farrant and I – that he was never going to get out until he wanted to. Not much more than a week previously he had made a botch of his last Test innings, and positively ruined his overall average, by untypically allowing himself to be bowled for a duck by Eric Hollies. Therefore, if anything at all was certain in cricket it was that he would not make an equal mess of his last appearance at Lord's.

At the Oval against Hollies he had shown human frailty; today he was infallible and so when his 50 came and later his hundred they were attended by such an air of inevitability that we greeted them like confidently-expected guests, with pleasure but no surprise.

Somewhere along the line he achieved another record to add to the multitude he already owned by becoming the only overseas player to score more than 2,000 runs on each of four tours of England. And a little after that he reached 150, and with a neat sense of timing decided to call it a day.

Freddie Brown was bowling to him – Freddie Brown who, throughout the Australian innings trundled with honest endeavour through 27 overs without achieving a single maiden – and perhaps

Bradman took pity on him. In any event slowly and gently he lofted the ball into the air, so slowly and gently that it could have been deliberate, so slowly and gently that, whatever the batsman's motive, it was almost sadistic, an underlining of the fact that the only man on the field that day who could get Bradman out was Bradman.

Martin Donnelly moved easily to the catch but well before he took it Bradman had removed his gloves, tucked his bat under his arm and begun walking back to the pavilion as briskly as he had left it.

Once again we all stood up and applauded and cheered, and for a long time after he had gone through the gate and up the steps and vanished for ever from our sight we were still clapping and cheering and Farrant beside me said: 'Gosh,' and I said nothing because suddenly I realized I was weeping.

Farrant said, accusingly: 'Norman, you're blubbing.'

I said: 'So are you, Farrant,' and so he was and so were most of the people around us. But they were all smiling, too, as if they couldn't quite work out which emotion had them in its grip.

Well, as we settled down and blew our noses and cleared our throats the game went on. Hassett, who had already shared a century stand with Bradman and eventually made 200 not out, was now joined by Keith Miller and these two put on another 100-odd for the fourth wicket. At close of play the Australians were 478 for three, but though I stayed to the end and watched every ball I have not the slightest recollection of either Hassett or Miller.

I just remember that Bradman had come to Lord's for the last time and scored 150. And I had seen it.

MAIDEN OVER
LAWRENCE DURRELL

His education in Darjiling, London and Canterbury ensured that he was never far from a cricket field. Later he went to live in Corfu where his love of cricket was nourished further, and in Prospero's Cell, a pastoral idyll set in the island, he has written about the game.

What is so peculiarly magical about cricket if it isn't its strange appropriateness to the landscape in which, and probably from which, it has sprung? Or is mine simply the reaction of a Colonial sensibility raised on the dry and featureless plains of the Indian sub-continent? At any rate, for me the very word England seems to echo with the image of green fields and forests skirmished all too often with a sweet spring rain – with the eloquent greenness of summer lawns and flawless cricket pitches where the solitary groundsman prowls at dawn like God the Father, pausing from time to time to pat a patch of sheer melodious green and pour down upon it the fruit of his deepest anxiety and concern. And of course cloudless skies – though these are all too rare in conscience! But cricket is quite something special in its grave and introspective nature, its decorous unfoldings; it never makes an appeal to the baser emotions, it provides a philosophic basis of acceptance for both defeat and victory. This secret hint of an esoteric philosophy of sport and sporting conduct as a surrogate for war and baser dealing must be what has secretly so intrigued foreigners, for long after the departure of the British Raj the game lingered on in India, in Cyprus, even in Corfu of all places! Trinidad? Tobago?

Yes, in the subconscious of every public schoolboy lurks the memory of those far off white-clad elevens of his youth (why 'elevens', one wonders) crossing and recrossing in the green meadows of summer in silences ever so faintly puckered by the clicking of bats and balls. Surely there is some ancient Roman mathematical mystery about the almost liturgical movements of these costumed figures whose whole attention is devoted to the quiet ritual of 'the game'?

'But his Captain's hand on his shoulder smote –
"Play up! Play up! and play The Game!"'

We were all very much alive to the ethical message propounded by the sacred game, and in almost every school mag. there was an article on 'the message of cricket'. It was a basic test of character in the Roman sense. One's sporting disposition, diagnosed through one's attitude to the game, determined whether one was virtuous or not. After all at a public school we were raised like young lions on the Roman poets and historians, on Livy and Plutarch and Ovid... *dulce et decorum est*... and so on!

But it must not be thought that this was a class matter, an expression of privilege and riches – quite the contrary. The whole country was bemused by the mystique of King Willow as he was sometimes poetically called in the popular press. The emergence and pre-eminence of county cricket had spread the taste and the preoccupation with cricket scores to the whole country, and even where there was no green grass to illustrate the poetry of it, as in the London slums, it was none the less ever-present as a concern, witness the chalked wickets one found on every grey factory wall or abandoned building site. Yes, the old gentleman ruled over the English subconscious with a rare authority; I can think of no other such example unless perhaps the prevalence of the game of *boules* in Provence. It also punctuates the silences of the woods with its meditative clicking noise. But it has not carried as far geographically as the English obsession has, though there is no reason why not.

At any rate even my Indian childhood was coloured by the talk of the Planter's Club in Darjiling where the problem of a green grass cricket pitch was a frequent and fervent topic which engaged my father's attention. *Indian grass was no good for cricket, it was far too coarse.* Attempts had been made to send out our own homegrown grass in turf slices but it had not worked; the grass tired quickly on the voyage and in the Indian heats simply turned to a dusty simulacrum of its English self. One had been forced to compromise with an artificial pitch of matting, but this gave one a rather dead surface, robbing the bowler of velocity and spin and tingle. Of course all this talk was quite fascinating for the Indians who were puzzled by so weird a national anachronism. Everything else about us was fairly clear to them – it was obvious for example that almost the whole of the English attitude to life was primitive and infantile, sometimes rather endearingly so; but there we were, servants of the Raj, tip-toeing about with a heavy unctuous preoccupied air, governess-worshippers to a man. It was uncanny! The national ethos with its picturesque anality was spiritually precarious and medically extremely unsound (drink, national egotism): indeed at times it seemed a sort of wilful clowning. But cricket on the other hand... what the *devil* was the secret buried in cricket? When they tried it, of course, they succumbed at once to its charms and stopped trying to analyse it. India gave cricket some of the giants of the game like Ranjitsinhji, to mention only one of them! Yes, for them the English were eccentric through and through, so be it! Perhaps Noel Coward had hinted at a new foreign Upanishad in his *Mad Dogs and Englishmen*?

For me life went on in the shadow of the great game for it had even invaded language and given us a yardstick with which to measure *moeurs*. Shady behaviour was 'not quite cricket', and everybody decent tried to keep 'a straight bat' as far as behaviour was concerned. Not always successfully. Sometimes like Bertie Wooster one was 'retired hit wicket' or simply 'out first ball' in matters of ordinary day-to-day living. And while I am on the topic I must not forget to mention old Brigadier Mainwaring, the soldier who was my boss for a spell in the Dodecanese Islands where the Army did a brief spell of caretaking before the Peace Conference. I was part of the administration which he inherited and he was terrified to hear that his press officer was one of those 'writer fellers', though mercifully not with long hair trailing down his back.

The old Brig, as he was affectionately called by his adoring staff, was a difficult man not to love, even to worship. His goodness of heart shone out like a beacon; he was utterly without guile or malevolence of any sort. He was goodness personified. In addition to this he was as shy as a kitten and blushed pink when confronted with a lady to talk to. Well, the Brig decided to sort out his staff and test everyone for character by his simple rule-of-thumb method which had always yielded a clear answer to his question. At last it came to the turn of the 'writer feller', and I saw that the Brig was though shy quite resolute in his resolve to plumb the depths of my soul. He stroked his moustache and talked of other things in a distracted sort of way until the right moment came. Then he said: 'I wonder if I could put to you a Personal Question which I have always considered to be the Absolute Acid Test of English character?' I wondered what on earth could be coming. 'You do not need to answer if you don't want to,' he went on, winding and unwinding his fingers. 'This is a democracy after all!' I signified my willingness to collaborate with him and after a long pause he said, darting me a raking look worthy of Holmes: 'Tell me one thing and one thing only, my boy. *Do you like village cricket?*'

I was able to reply in perfect sincerity: 'Brigadier, I worship village cricket!' at which he exploded with relief, blowing out his cheeks and almost crossing himself. 'I say, how ripping! What a very good show!' he went on, now quite reassured about his press officer. It was the beginning of a perfect friendship, for from then on when there was nothing much to do the Brig enjoyed having me round for a little chat about cricket. He even had plans to start up cricket once more in Rhodes but alas time proved too short. But anyway I was able to boast to him of several unique cricket experiences I had had as a schoolboy. I had been present at the Oval when Hobbs made his hundreth hundred and crowd-frenzy almost broke loose to celebrate the event. The great batsman even gave me his autograph – 'J.B. Hobbs' in a neat copperplate hand. On another occasion I had seen Larwood dealing out his infamous bodyline bowling to the Australians – bringing dishonour on the game, I thought, for it intruded the notion of violence and physical harm to the batsman. It wasn't cricket, strictly speaking. It was most unsporting conduct.

The Brig rather shared my views about the matter; indeed as far as *cricket* was concerned we saw eye to eye in most things – except perhaps in the superior subtlety of left-handed spin bowlers, as exemplified by men like Woolley. Best of all, in the cellars of the old town library I came on a secret hoard of juvenile books and papers left behind by who knows what youth club, with among them a few copies of the ancient *Magnet* in which

were recounted the marvellous matches played by Harry Wharton and Bob Cherry as leading batsmen for the Greyfriars School First Eleven some time before the Flood. What a pleasure to resavour the prose of my old friend Frank Richards who was my first prose model – the creator of Billy Bunter and other marvellous literary carnival figures! The Brig was in Heaven and I think he would have put me up for a gong if I had so wished.

I was lucky to have two English schooldays, the first in the heart of Shakespeare's Cockney London in the shadow of Tower Bridge. Here we played slum cricket on asphalt but real cricket in East Dulwich on the beautiful greensward of Alleyn's School. In my second schoolboy incarnation it was Canterbury, at St Edmund's Clergy Orphan school whose buildings were as beautiful as if they had been designed by Ruskin and William Morris in concert. The playground was a beautiful thing, complete with a small pavilion like a Japanese temple. When not playing one could lie around in the deep grass with a bag of cherries and perhaps a copy of Donne's love poems to help tide over the sleepier patches of the match.

I was always a poor Latinist otherwise I should have tried to find a Roman pedigree for the game of cricket, for I think it seems of Roman provenance, it is so much of a rite, perhaps a spring rite? I wonder also whether I could not have found its ancestry in terms of a tree-goddess, patron of the Willow tree from which our bats were fashioned. I am sure such a nymph existed and that a little research could uncover her name! It would be well worth trying on behalf of cricketers to come!

MY CAREER IN CRICKET

ROBIN BAILEY

His deepest cricketing associations are with the Nottinghamshire of Larwood and Voce. In a varied career in theatre, films and television, his many dressing-rooms in Australia as well as England have served as happy meeting-places for cricket lovers and heroes of the game. Lately he has been much concerned with the characters of the Brigadier in _Tales from a Long Room_ and of Charters, who endlessly argues about _Wisden_ statistics with his friend Mr Caldicott.

On summer evenings in the late Twenties, after his work for the day at Trent Bridge was over, Harold Larwood frequently dismissed the entire Australian side for less than twenty runs. His action during these triumphs would not have been recognizable to Neville Cardus. Even with the coal-place door open the back-yard of Number 10 Watnall Road, Hucknall allowed insufficient space for a run-up and he was bowling slow, underarm leg-breaks, but they were more than Woodfull, Ponsford, Bradman and their team-mates could cope with. They seemed to have no defence. If the ball missed the rather vaguely defined area of the brick wall which represented the wicket they were allowed one run, but a slightly more accurate delivery meant they were out. Sometimes if, say, McCabe seemed to be offering resistance, Bill Voce would be called on to take over – usually with instant success.

This was the beginning of my career in cricket and I was off to a flying start. I was Larwood. And I was also Voce.

These were Camelot cricket days when it seemed almost never to rain till after sun-down, but if it did there was still no escape for the Australians. There was always book-cricket involving the use of a code which translated the initial letter of any page of _Just William_ or _Treasure Island_ into cricketing terms. R=1 run, S=stumped, Y=bowled, and so on. I suppose the scorecard might more fairly have read: 'O'Reilly c

Richmal Crompton b R.L. Stevenson' but it never did. It was always 'c
Voce b Larwood' or 'c Larwood b Voce.' And I was always Larwood. And
I was always Voce.

And my success had been achieved without coaching. Miss
Molloy, Headmistress of Beardall Street Infants School, did not include
sporting activities in her curriculum, and I never saw Miss Piggin or Miss
Webster padded up.

So I was not well prepared when I moved eventually to a senior
school with grass and nets, and an expectation of overarm bowling at a
wicket twenty-two yards away. I tried to reproduce the leg-breaks that had
been so successful against the Australians but, delivered from round the
back of the neck, line and length were not easy to control. However, my
first ball completely beat the bat of Mr S.R. Revill (History and Sarcasm)
and I thought it was ungracious of him, as he handed over the two pennies
I had knocked off his stumps, to tell me: 'I don't call a ball that bounces
about six times, a ball at all, Bailey.' Further discouragement came from
Mr H. (Nemo) Newitt (Latin and Sadism) and it became clear that if I was
to proceed with a career in cricket I would have to approach it obliquely;
round the wicket in fact.

Local walks took me often past the houses of my heroes: past
Butler's Hill to Bill Voce's, up to Annesley Road to Harold Larwood's, and
eventually through arrangements made by Paddy Griffin the High Street
barber (Men's haircut 6d, Boys 3d) I was invited to the Voces for tea and
sat beside the great man as he showed me his silver-plated trophies.

I went to Trent Bridge as often as I could and sometimes to the
pretty ground further down the Loughborough Road owned by Sir Julien
Cahn who use to bowl, as someone once decribed, not so much 'up and
down' as 'to and fro'; at the same time wearing a cap, two sweaters and a
blazer. I saw him leading a team of distinguished players, sometimes
choosing to open the innings and sometimes to close it but invariably
scoring runs and always, but always, winning.

It was indirectly through Sir Julien that some years later my
cricketing career took another step forward. He had developed a second
cricket-ground at Stanford Hall, his country home near Loughborough.
He had added to the Hall an extra wing to accommodate and indulge his
two particular pleasures which were conjuring and cricket. So the ground
floor was a theatre where he would perform his tricks for the delight of his
captive guests and the upper storey was divided into twelve rooms for the
team and presumably an umpire, whose night's accommodation, I
suspect, might well have been dependent on the generosity of his decisions
during the day. All I had to do to win two weeks of luxury at Stanford Hall
was to contract appendicitis while on war-time leave from the Army, by
which time the wing had been given over to the Red Cross and the only
guests wearing white were the nurses. So, although I never quite made Sir

Julien's team, I did spend a fortnight in one of their beds – and how many sporting journalists could boast as much?

To advance my career still further I decided to marry into cricket. My prospective bride had told me that as a small girl she had been waltzed round a dance-floor by Herbert Sutcliffe. So, in the manner of the Herbert Farjeon song, I can claim that I've danced with a girl, who danced with a man, who danced down the wicket with Hobbs.

So far, so good; but I was ambitious and progress was slow. I had to make another positive move if I was ever to be invited to tour Australia. I decided to take up work in the theatre.

For some years it seemed that the covers might never be taken off again as far as my career was concerned. Not a ball was bowled, for instance, during a run of *Murder in the Cathedral,* and while many other dramas opened and closed, Play never Commenced.

Eventually, however, my strategy was seen to be working, and in Melbourne, during a theatrical success, I was asked to address the sixth form of a boys' school. I reported to the Headmaster's office and read the name on the door: W.M. WOODFULL. I believe I was tactless enough to mention the name 'Larwood' but was careful to avoid any reference to my many moments of triumph in unrecorded battles long ago.

In Sydney I had invited guests to a performance of *My Fair Lady.* Since they were no ordinary guests they came to the dressing-room before the performance, and when he heard the traditional call of 'Five Minutes Please' Mr Larwood said to Mrs Larwood: 'Come on, then. Let's leave him to it. I know what it's like. It's like looking out of t'pavilion windows and watching them umpires going out in their white coats, and you get them butterflies.' I felt I was back on course.

There were many other visitors to the dressing-room during that time and none more welcome, of course, than the Australian cricketers and visiting teams from the West Indies and England. One of the visitors lingered one evening after a performance and eventually asked me would I, as a personal favour, stress a particular final consonant. How could I refuse? Others have abandoned the reverse sweep and given up flashing outside the off-stump for the same man. Yes, Peter. Of course, Mr May.

Perhaps it was due to such contact with the hierarchy of the MCC, and my willingness to co-operate, that I finally played for England. It wasn't at the Gabba or the Oval, nor at Perth or Headingley. It was on the lawn of a house in Kent where I was the guest of Mr P.E. Richardson of Worcestershire, Kent and England. Following a Sunday lunch, Peter's sons and their friends were fitted with Australian caps collected in the course of various Test series, and Peter and I wore England caps. I played two quite distinguished innings and finished with an average of 8.5, which was rather higher than the average of the opposing side. Of their ages I mean.

Since then I have to admit there have been fallow periods such as most cricketers suffer, but the strong survive.

My activities in television have lately been much concerned with the 'summer game' in the adopted persona of Peter Tinniswood's Brigadier and as Hugo Lovelace Charters arguing about *Wisden* statistics with his friend Mr Caldicott. I don't feel I can claim any personal cricketing credit on that account, but I do claim this – only last year I travelled up four floors of a Manchester hotel with Mr I.V.A. Richards. As I stepped out of the lift, I heard him distinctly say: 'Good night'.

That's what I call success.

A CHILD'S CRICKET IN LANCASHIRE

HENRY GRAHAM

Has published several books of poems and appeared in many anthologies. He is a poetry editor of the literary magazine _Ambit_ (London), and lectures on the Arts for Liverpool Polytechnic. Once an enthusiastic cricketer (see poems), he now confines himself entirely to the role of spectator.

In 1947–48 I played with and for Bootle CC at Wadham Rd, Liverpool, at the time Leary Constantine was occasionally there. These poems celebrate nostalgically then and now.

I

The past
like a scattering of lost
cricket balls
in the long summer grass.
In the long summer passed,
before boredom and whisky
and work took their toll,
a lad of seventeen
played the game
with the men on the square
of life, at the centre
of the forever oval world.

What has passed
is an urgent innocence
an absolute necessity
to win at all cost;
no one is ever
not out in this game
at the last.

II

One term
at my school I achieved
a half century
of absences. Playing truant
at the nets with cricketers
more able than I
seemed more profitable than
geometry or pi.

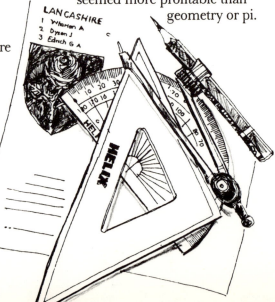

And I am sure I found
more of life
in those forever dwindling
never ending days in the sun,
more about accepting
an end and how to begin;
and more about
these middle years, how to take
a run out without expecting
justice or a pat on the back.

III

At night in light snow
under sodium lighting
two intent figures
at the nets without nets
in the centre of a road.

To be that dedicated
is the most extraordinary thing
or so it seems to me today.
To be that keen to accelerate
performance, to make the team
and keep one's place
has never been repeated, well
not by me at any rate.
Life then was to drink
from an ever brimming cup.
Now if at first I don't
succeed, I give up.

IV

When Learie
and the black men came
to Wadham Road, they were
the rarest sight
I'd ever seen.
For us all there had never
been such exotic
supple creatures, such explosive
laughter on the green
of our ground, and such
a game.

And I shook
the great man's hand,
he bowled to me
and I to him, never
was there such a net
as that day
or ever since. And he
stayed on, he joined us
and sometimes
he played with the team.
Now of course
all seems but a fading dream.

V

Lancashire the county
of the greats,
the greatest exponents
of the game. And Yorkshire?
We tried not to think
about Yorkshire. The red rose
had to grow upon my cap,
no other desire, not even
girls could keep me from it.

The nearest I came –
much later playing jazz
with a horn playing wicket
keeper from Old Trafford;
the best I could do.

And now nothing left
but memories
of a setting sun, sounds
and smells across
the shadowed field,
white on green, my hands
held out for the catch
that never came.

THE EPITHETS
TIM RICE

Founder and captain of Heartaches CC. *This club was created in 1973 when he realized that nobody else would pick him. Since then the lads in red, pink and green have gone from strength to strength, occasionally winning matches. Now and then Mr Rice (amateur!) is distracted from his cricketing activities by the theatre as his contribution to such pieces as Joseph and the Amazing Technicolour Dreamcoat, Jesus Christ Superstar, Evita, Blondel and Chess will testify. He is also a book publisher (Pavilion Books) and author (The Guinness Book of British Hit Singles, etc).*

The strain of captaining a side such as my own distinguished XI, Heartaches CC, can leave its mark on the most relaxed of leaders if he is not careful. More often than not it is the problems of selection rather than the worries on the actual field of play that age the amateur skipper – these can take days rather than minutes to resolve and an ill-judged selection (or rejection) can wreck friendships, million-pound business deals and/or marriages (many a cricketer's home life has been put to the severest of tests when the call of family duty is put up against the call of the willow). Small wonder that in the winter months I spend many a happy hour selecting teams whose members never complain, let me down, abuse, misuse or confuse me – mainly because these sides are imaginary only; often dominated by players from the past or from fiction. Let me tell you about the Epithets.

All cricket lovers have chosen their World XI team to play Mars and since the days of Fuller Pilch and John Wisden literally millions of other intriguing but non-existent teams must have been picked by selectors of all ages and of all times. Teams consisting of men whose surnames begin with a particular letter of the alphabet, teams of men all born under one astrological sign, teams from one particular era, or teams whose members share some unusual characteristic, such as those who turned out (a real match, this) in the fixture reported in the 1868 *Wisden* (p.86), One Arm v One Leg (match drawn); these and many more colourful combinations have flickered to and fro across the daydreams of gentlemen and players, and always will. The most fascinating side I have ever selected is the Epithets – and as you all know, the Oxford Dictionary defines an epithet as a 'significant appellation.'

I have a good friend in the music world called Mike Batt, a distinguished composer whose most famous song is probably *Bright Eyes*. Although recently married to an Australian, Mike has shown little interest when I have suggested that he becomes part of a cricket XI that I have been trying to organize for some time. This is a team of players whose every member's name is either a crucial item required for a game of cricket, or a vital aspect or skill of the game. Mike Batt (spelling inconsistencies are permitted) is a natural choice for this side, if not for the captaincy itself (this is earmarked for a German friend of mine named Franz Lieder). I have several other chums who would qualify for this bizarre assembly, but like Mike, they seem to have been put off cricket for life by the close association with the great game forced upon them from day one as a result of an accident of birth. A colleague from my schooldays was called Padd (presumably, he still is) and I have shared an office in my time with both a Mr Slipp and Mr Court. These men are as one with Batt in their loathing for cricket.

It is therefore likely to take me some time to get this team together. I am forced to turn to history and here my task is easier; but not that much more easy, for there have been comparatively few cricketers of distinction who would qualify for this wacky outfit. I have decreed that the team should be exclusively English and drawn only from those who have played first-class cricket. The English rule is a bit rough on eminent foreign internationals such as G.M. Guard (India) and J.B. Plimsoll (South Africa) who would have been a useful, if not sensational, opening pace attack, but I am afraid I can only bring myself to dedicate my selectorial time to Englishmen. Anyway I am sure experts will agree that there would be no room for both a Boot and a Plimsoll in the side.

Here are the Epithets, as selected – the result of many hours of research and painstaking deliberation:
Green, Studd, Legge, Bowling, Box, Bale, Ball, Major (capt.), Close, Fielder, Boot. Twelfth man: Remnant. Umpire: Judge. Scorer: Scorer. How would this lot fare against (say) a similar side from India, selected by Contractor? Let us examine the form and background of the chosen few.

There would be nothing wrong with the opening partnership. The Green chosen to begin the Epithet assault is one of over a dozen Greens to qualify for selection. There are also several Greenes and Greenfields jostling for attention but the man I have chosen to represent

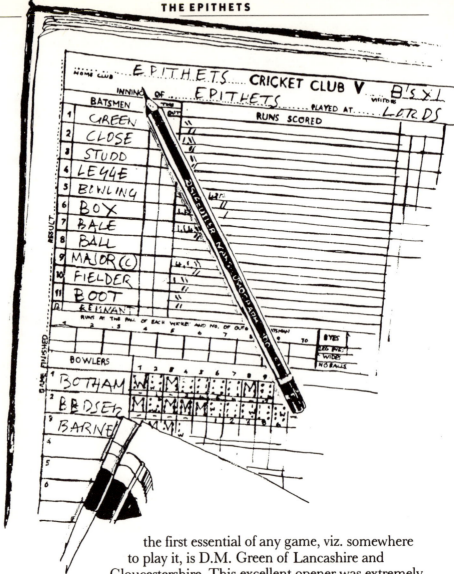

the first essential of any game, viz. somewhere to play it, is D.M. Green of Lancashire and Gloucestershire. This excellent opener was extremely unlucky never to have been chosen for England during his career, particularly in 1965 when he scored 2,000 runs without the aid of a single century and in 1968, when he averaged over 40, scoring his seasonal best total of 2,137. Still, it is far harder to win a place in the Epithets and I trust that this honour will more than compensate for the injustices meted out to him by the England selectors. His partner has to be the indestructible Brian Close, of whose breathless hush Sir Henry Newbolt waxed poetic. Close's career as an inspired and fearless all-rounder has spanned five decades and is not finished yet (1985). Now at last he has a side for whom he can go on playing forever.

After this scenic start, we come down to less picturesque but still vital components of cricket. At the critical position of number three, C.T. Studd (Middlesex) is chosen to remind us that even the tiniest details of the game are of crucial importance. No man in this side will slip as he turns for a quick second run. It would have been possible for me to have picked nine Studds, nearly two Boots' worth, but I did not want to skimp in my coverage of other departments of the game. C.T. was the most talented of the Studd family, topping the first-class averages in 1882 and playing five times for England, which is why he is the Studd I have collared.

Above Studd on the body but one below him in the order is G.B. Legge of Kent and England, who lost his life in World War II. This stylish batsman will, I'm glad to say, live on at number four for the Epithets. His slow bowling and alert slip fielding will also be invaluable. It did not take long to decide that Legge was a better bet than any of the three Legards who could have been chosen. Besides, leg-guard is now an obsolete term. (No first-class Padd exists.)

Following Legge is K. Bowling of Lancashire. His selection is a bit of a long shot, but so was Tyson's in 1954. Bowling only played once, for Lancashire, in that very same year, 1954. Confusingly, he played as a batsman but scored only seven runs in his two knocks. Lancashire never asked him back but I, remembering such successful shock selections as Washbrook v Australia in 1956 and Steele v Australia in 1975, have. No Bowler qualifies for selection, and the two potential Bowles are not quite right – I am looking for nouns rather than verbs.

It would be a rash man indeed who embarked upon an innings without a Box, and I am not about to break with tradition. Thos. Box played for Sussex, Surrey and Hampshire for more than thirty years in the middle of the last century, and so adds a wealth of experience to his crucial protective role. He was a fine wicket-keeper and middle-order batsman. However I do not propose to burden him with work behind the timbers; his job for the Epithets is to score well at number six.

I have every faith in my first six batsmen to get us off to a good start, and indeed it is vital that they do, for there is not a lot left after the opposition have got past Box. At number seven, perhaps batting a little above his station, is Frank Bale of Leicestershire. He was considered an all-rounder of great promise in the early 1920s, but he never quite fulfilled the hopes others had of him. Maybe in these new colours he will feel more relaxed and able to show his full potential. He is the second left-handed batsman in the order (Close of course being the other) and his left-arm slows will be handy.

Several Balls are available; none, sad to say, a leading player of his time. But so vital is a Ball to any game that a place must be found for at least one and the Ball chosen in the hope that he will last for a whole match is K.J. of Northants. He made only twelve first-class appearances, in 1921, but even that is more than any other English Ball. He was a middle-order batsman and a change bowler who might just come good at number eight, one ahead of his captain, L.H. Major. Major is a little lucky to lead the Epithets in that there has never been a first-class English Captain or Skipper, and the only other qualified Major was a professional and thus clearly unsuitable for the leadership of a side such as this. Still, L.H. was felt to be a 'useful' bowler when he made his debut for Somerset in 1903. A pity that his first match was also his last – until now.

At number ten is (at last) another Test player, Arthur Fielder of Kent. He toured Australia twice, in 1903–4 and 1907–8. He played six Tests in all, and took all 10 wickets in an innings for the Players v Gentlemen in 1906. A fast bowler of undoubted quality, he once scored a century batting at number eleven which is why I have no hesitation in promoting him now to the dizzy heights of number ten.

The career of the number eleven, Jesse Boot of Derbyshire, is in stark contrast to that of Fielder. But where would a Fielder be without a Boot? Not only that, Boot is the side's stumper, having kept wicket in his one match back in 1895, holding two catches. I am sure many more await him as a Epithet.

The twelfth man has to be a Remnant and George Henry (Kent) just gets the vote over his son, Ernest Richard, and over the aristocratic duo of the Hon. Peter Remnant and the Hon. Robert Remnant. The latter became the second Baron Remnant in 1933, but even this up-market achievement cannot oust G.H. from the substitute's bench. The favoured Remnant was not only a competent fast round-arm bowler in the late nineteenth century but also lived well into his own nineties, an indication that he possesses stamina and patience in spades. The team's umpire has to be the only Judge ever to have graced the first-class circuit, the Middlesex pre-World War II amateur, P.F., and for Scorer one need look no further than R.I. Scorer (Warwickshire 1921–26). The baggage master would be the brilliantly christened C.C.C. Case who played 255 matches for Somerset from 1925 to 1935 as a defensive middle-order batsman.

There is no Batt, Batsman or Batter in this squad, and players such as Hooker, Driver and Pullar narrowly miss selection because their names are too specialized. Similarly, players who describe merely particular styles of bowling such as Sloman, Speed and Shuter are, with reluctance, deemed ineligible. A fielder such as Spiller would be a bad choice on several counts. Nonetheless I feel the Epithets would give a reasonable account of themselves against most other teams of the imagination; maybe an XI of H's (Hobbs, Hendren, Hammond, Hutton....) or B's (Bradman, Barnes, Bedser, Botham...) would be a tough proposition, but I would back the Epithets to slaughter Heartaches CC any day.

A MEASURE OF NOSTALGIA
LORD HOME OF THE HIRSEL

Played cricket for Eton and at times for Oxford University, though missed a Blue. Also played once for Middlesex and went on tour with P. F. Warner to South America. Since 1920 has seen nearly all the great cricketers in action; watching them has been one of his happiest relaxations.

Nostalgia is a dangerous drug, but I confess to indulgence in the cricket season, when hankering after some of the features of the game of sixty years ago.

When I began to play in the Twenties the fast bowlers would direct 99 per cent of their deliveries between middle and leg and the off stump with the result that the wicket-keeper stood up to them. I recall Mervyn Hill, for example, at Eton and Cambridge, standing up to G. O. Allen, and he was very quick. It was generally a satisfying and exciting affair, and the occasional stumping on the leg-side was one of the most stylish achievements in the game. Nor did the Strudwicks and Co have a longstop – nor were the extras high.

In such circumstances to bowl outside the legs was positively bad form, and the bowler didn't last long who did so.

The result, in terms of style, was that the off-side strikes, the cover and straight drives, the square and late cuts prevailed, with the pulled drive and the hook for the bowler who pitched short. The captain, with a thin leg-side field, could not afford to keep such a bowler on for long.

The adoption of the leg theory and its extravagant body-line technique undoubtedly did a lot of damage to the game as a spectacle, for it tucked up even the best of batsmen, and the spectators became bored to such a point that the rules had to be changed. As a result the batsman is again given a chance to show his skill and style and the crowds respond.

There is another revival which I welcome without reserve. It is the return of spin. It has always had its special place among the virtues with me, ever since Canon Edward Lyttelton confessed that he could never walk up the nave of his Cathedral 'without speculating whether it would take spin'.

Cricket, like everything else, has its fashions, but why for so long the cult of swing was adopted, and spin ignored, is a mystery. The seamer is estimable and deserves his place in the cricket side, but not at both ends all the time.

The spinners of old – O'Reilly, Grimmett and Freeman – added enormously to the fascination of the game, for they tempted the batsman to disaster, and that the public always enjoys.

Of course, one-day cricket was always the order of the day for school and club cricket, and there is nothing wrong with that. I confess that I still hanker after the elasticity of the declaration, rather than the automatic application of the numbers of overs bowled. The captain who had to calculate to a nicety the time which his bowlers would require to get the other side out, faced a constant challenge in tactics in which the spectators shared.

Certainly, exciting results are achieved by the present method, but I would prefer the flexibility of human success or error which the declaration involves.

When one-day cricket is brought up to the county or national level its benefit to the players is much more doubtful. True, it draws the crowds, and true it also is (if deplorable) that money matters more and more. However, I cannot believe that for the middle batsmen it can improve their performance or their prospects as batsmen of class if they have to bat against time. Cash matters so much to the counties that the one-day contests will have to continue, but I would shed no tears at all if they were dropped at Test match level.

Finally, I cannot say that I like the accompaniment of noise at the modern Test match. It seems at variance with the peace of a summer day; but if that is the price of attracting the young to watch the game it is a small one to pay, provided always that, in return for that indulgence, they will agree that the essence of cricket is good manners.

Given that, I can discard my nostalgia and enjoy the best of games.

GET LOST, WURWURS'
PAUL JENNINGS

A man who has always been in love with cricket but was jilted by the game at an early age. Born with a lazy eye, he found his cricketing satisfaction in the scorebox with only rare incursions on to the field of play.

I came rather late (i.e. about twenty years after everybody else who reads the kinds of books that used to be known as 'seminal') to *Games People Play*, by the American (of course) Eric Berne, MD (well, it *says* MD on the jacket). Imagine my rage when I found, as early as page 16, a section called 'The Structuring of Time', after I, who am clearly never going to be a popular-psychiatry or any other kind of best-seller, had been saying for more than *forty* years that the English discovered the answer to this fundamental problem of human life, how to get through time without being intellectual, going mad, or simply killing people (either individually, like Dr Crippen, or collectively, in war) in their creation of the sublime game of cricket.*

In this section Eric Berne, MD writes: '... in everyday terms, what can people do after they have exchanged greetings, whether the greeting consists of a collegiate "Hi!" or an Oriental ritual lasting several hours? After stimulus-hunger and recognition-hunger comes *structure-hunger*.' God bless us all, what does the good Doctor imagine the English were doing in the period between, roughly, 1750 and 1850? Everybody knows that we had the Industrial Revolution that changed the world for ever; Napoleon's armies could move no faster than Caesar's, but the next major ones, Grant's and Lee's, could be moved in trains – and all the devices from which this clanking, whirring, ever-faster modern world was born, from Arkwright's spinning-frame in 1769 to Stephenson's *Rocket* triumph in 1829, were invented and developed in these islands. But another (and deeper) part of our national psyche realized that we were not put into the world to make more things more cheaply than anyone else. We stumbled

---

*I am not for a moment suggesting that *we* didn't have wars too. But many of them were to stop people like Napoleon and the Kaiser and Hitler from getting too big for their boots and running a world in which there would be no cricket.

33

on this barbarous and destructive process by a geographical-historical accident, and we have *never* really believed in it. We *never* stood by our machines and sang company songs like the Japanese. We had the first machines – and the first Luddites.

In exactly the same period we also developed cricket, a far more beautiful and artistic answer to the whole thing than mere Ludditism. It is the *opposite* of the Industrial Revolution. It is a way of doing nothing, of filling time creatively, not by sitting round Left Bank café tables and going on endlessly about Essence and Being and structuralism and the rest of it (or even, to do the French justice, playing *boules*, a simple grown-up version of marbles). Cricket can fill five whole days, if necessary. It has formal, sophisticated, highly developed rules and a rhythm as inexorable as the tide – six balls this way, six balls that. Yet within this classical structure, what regard for the dignity of human individuality – the solemn change-over of the field every time a left-hander takes strike, the umpires' subsidiary function as clothes-horses for sweaters, the intervals, especially the tea interval: how right it seemed for the policeman at Headingley guarding the wicket during one such, to have some himself, at a little table with waitress service.

Mind you, a mere twenty years ago the idea of policemen having to guard the wicket or anything else would have been inconceivable. It is only recently that the Wurwurs have insinuated their evil presence even into cricket. The name is derived from the dreadful bawling wordless hymns they sing (though one may sometimes catch the single word ING-LUND):

> '*Wur wur, wur wur, wur WUR wur wur*
> *Wur wur wur wur WUR,*' etc.

It is a much apter word than *hooligan*, which implies a certain larkiness out of which young men eventually grow up. Wurwurs never grow up. There's no need here to go into the harm hooligans and wurwurs between them have done to the good name of Ing-lund in soccer. Of course we taught the world *that* too, and much more thoroughly and completely, back in the good old pre-wurwur days. But it's worth noting that the only *royal* cricket club in the world, in Holland, got its *Koninklijke* title in 1958, when it was already seventy-five years old; that Philadelphia beat Sussex and Warwickshire and drew with Yorkshire in 1897, and indeed there are those who think that baseball only supplanted cricket as America's summer game in the Civil War, when soldiers had to play this developed version of rounders on any chance bit of rough ground they could find in landscapes not over-endowed with rolled, pampered, carefully tended wickets.

All the same, I hope that the non-American English-speaking peoples who are our main opponent-partners in this wonderful game will not take it amiss when I say that in spite of certain benefits that their fiery enthusiasm, so different from the polite Anglican ripple of applause under the lengthening shadow of great elm trees (*elms*! O, my vanished elms!) and murmurs of 'Well played, sir!' the limited-over one-day games (and, dare I say it, their own versions of wurwurism) have brought to cricket, it remains more quintessentially English than any other game.

It has in some mysterious way to do with names. No-one would deny that Bradman or Lillee are perfectly apt-sounding cricket surnames, as for that matter are Kapil Dev or Learie Constantine (and, better still, *Sir* Learie Constantine, *Sir* Len Hutton, *Prince* Ranjitsinhji); or that men with names like F. R. Spofforth or H. Trumble were destined, fated, *born* to be Australia's greatest early bowlers in the same way as no-one called Sarson is really fulfilling himself unless he runs a vinegar factory or the day Chatto met Windus they must have said, in the same breath: 'Let us publish books.'

But these are as nothing compared with the way the great foundation-names of cricket are inextricably intertwined with the deepest roots of English national consciousness. *Hambledon* (as resonant as and consonant with *Wimbledon*), the first club in the world, had its games on *Broadhalfpenny* and *Windmill Downs*. When it ended in 1791 the *Marylebone Cricket Club* (started in 1787) became the world authority as cricket moved from rural to metropolitan and national consciousness; Marylebone, with Madame Tussaud's, the Baker Street of Sherlock Holmes, the Wallace Collection, the great parish church where Browning was married, and now the Radio Times offices and oil sheikhs in their Rolls-Royces visiting Harley Street clinics – who would have thought its first ground was in Dorset Square, now a few urban trees glimpsed briefly on one's left on the mad one-way northward exit up Gloucester Place from the West End, soon to pass the very Tabernacle of cricket, *Lord's* itself? What could have a more quasi-Biblical sound of authority about it than the Book of *Wisden?*

What other game employing twenty-two men, of whom at any one time nine are sitting in a *pavilion*, would have the word *googly* to describe a ball, invented by B.J.T. Bosanquet, father of the late lamented TV news announcer, which a batsman skilled enough to recognize the wrist action of a bowler intending to make the ball break from his leg side, would be disconcerted to find breaking instead from the off, causing him to make a fumbling, late-decision attempt at some sort of drive and providing an easy catch? I looked up 'googly bowler' in the wonderful (German-produced) *Sports Dictionary in Seven Languages* (e.g. 'pole vault' is *salto con pertiga* in Spanish, *Stabhochsprung* in German, *salto con l'asta* in Italian and *rúdugrás* in Hungarian) and all it could offer was *servidor de 'googly'* (Spanish), *Googly-Baller* (German) and the magnificent Hungarian *'googly' dobásmódot alkalmazo dobó*. Can you wonder?

The name of B.J.T. Bosanquet is also a reminder of how effortlessly cricket harmonized itself with the social revolution, how painlessly it passed from the days of Gentlemen v Players, a surely unmissable target for the guns of radical satire but hardly ever fired at, when all Gentlemen had three initials and Professionals had none at all, even though already, in my schooldays, everyone just knew it was *Jack* Hobbs and *Herbert* Sutcliffe. And so, painlessly, to the days of Geoff Boycott, Mike Gatting, etc.

R.E.S. Wyatt, captain of Warwickshire (and, for that matter, England) was an old boy of my first school, King Henry VIII Coventry. The professional was simply Quaife. You had to be pretty close to him to know that he was Will Quaife, a great Warwickshire batsman in his day. In fact, just before typing this I was on the phone to another Old Coventrian, now a doctor, who was in a game with Quaife on his 66th birthday, in 1933, when he made 66 not out.

Many people who write pieces this long about cricket have by this time told you their best score, against whom, etc. As I was born with something called a lazy eye (my left one) and you need very good stereoscopic vision for cricket, it will be clear that my love for the game has not been returned in terms of mere achievement. At KHS you got an arrow which could be sewn on your school cap if you had attended more than a certain number of voluntary games on our Wednesday and Saturday half-holidays. The maximum number allowed was three; and I never had *less* than three. I was always in the bottom game (but ah, the special free atmosphere, the lemonade and sandwiches, the often rather surrealist larking about – in short, to quote Eric Berne, MD, the structuring of time!).

At my second school, Douai, the headmaster combined four incredible excellences: Dom Ignatius Rice was a Benedictine monk, an intimate friend of G. K. Chesterton (indeed, the only person other than Mrs Chesterton and Monsignor O'Connor, the original of Father Brown, present at GKC's reception into the Catholic Church), who had taken a First in Greats *and* played for Warwickshire. And surely not even Dr Grace himself strode out to the wicket with greater majesty than when I saw him do it probably for the last time (and for a regrettably low score, certainly nothing like 66).

I therefore find it hard to say which of my cricket memories, if you can call them that, I treasure most. On the one hand, I did make 13 not out for *The Observer* against *The News Of The World* (the only people we could play, on our free Mondays, were either other Sunday papers or the police, who in that carefree time could play on any day, instead of being bussed 100 miles to some riot of wurwurs); but we had already won anyway, and I think the *News of the World* people were just making a kind gesture to tail-enders with non-stereoscopic vision, like me.

On the other hand, it was *my* photograph at the top of the cricket section of the Douai school magazine for 1935 and 1936. Was I taken magically in hand by someone even greater than Quaife, you ask?

Alas (and well, also, hooray), no. I was the scorer.

THE CASE FOR THREE BAT HANDLES

COLIN WELLAND

Played cricket at school and college then moved on to Second Division Manchester Association, but only really saw the light when taught to swing the ball by a certain Mr Arnold at Surrey in the Sixties. Since then, has enjoyed bowling medium pace with the Lord's Taverners and Sparks. Still a keen watcher of the game, live and on TV, to the delight of young son and annoyance of wife.

As a kid I bowled spin. Playing in parks and on goal-mouth wickets, worn bare in the winter and baked hard in the summer, it was the only sensible thing to do. You could turn it like a dog's back leg on goal-area gravel, especially if the corky had a couple of well-picked holes in it, you know, to stick your fingers in. I remember bowling my Uncle Don (no mean batsman in the Liverpool Combination) with one that pitched a foot outside the off and took his leg stump. He still talks about it. It was a good job I *did* bowl him, for even though he'd gone down the wicket to me I'd no chance of a stumping. We never had a stumper, only a long stop...we never had any gloves, see! The tichiest or skinniest would be posted well back, armed with a coat to throw on the ball as it sped past. It stopped it going in the nettles. Anyway stumpings, run outs, lbw's and such were always hotly contested. Such disputes would be settled with 'three bat handles'...the batsman facing three balls with his bat reversed. If he survived – he survived – if you see what I mean. Tradition. As it was for the owner of bat, or ball, or both to go in last...to prevent him nipping off home when he'd had his innings. Not Marylebone Laws but just as effective, equally sacrosanct, and maybe stretching back down even longer years.

This padless, three-springered, insulating tape-bound, one-hand-off-the-wall world was my cricket heritage.

38

Since growing up I've played charity games on some of the best wickets in the country… But I've had to change to slow medium. Once you've bent it a couple of feet you can never be content with a couple of inches. I'm glad we can afford keepers' gloves now though – that helps with the thick edges. But I sometimes think as a batsman, judged lbw, sulks off in that thunderous gloom of injustice, that three bat handles still might not be a bad idea.

JUST FOR THE RECORD
HUMPHREY TILLING

Played for Tonbridge School 1st XI, for Old Tonbridgians and Yellowhammers and had two trials for Surrey as a leg-spinner, playing for one season in the County 2nd XI. Has performed with the Old Stagers at Canterbury Cricket Week for more than fifty years, and was their manager for thirty years; he is now president of the Society. As a player he also represented the Refreshers and Wonersh, batting on even after he couldn't see the fast ones; eventually gave up when he couldn't hear them either.

Few cricketers are the current holders of a world record. Even fewer, I guess, hold two. I claim, I think without much fear of contradiction, to be in the latter category.

The first was acquired on one of the world's most famous grounds – the Kennington Oval.

In those far-off days before the war, the Bar ran a cricket side. We called ourselves the Refreshers and played annually three matches against the Law Society, the Stage and the Barristers' Clerks. It was against the last-named that I attained my first record. Do not think that the Clerks had a side to be despised. They were full of good cricketers. Their captain, Reg Henty, would have graced any county side had he been able to afford the time to play regularly. In this particular match we won the toss and decided to bat. I went in first for the Bar, and had to receive the first ball, my opening companion having been called to the Bar some years before I was.

I strode out confidently from the pavilion, expecting to impress a number of High Court Judges who were among the spectators.

Reg opened the bowling for the Clerks. He bowled fast-medium stuff which often moved to the off-side off the wicket. As he ran up to the wicket to deliver his first ball it was obvious that something was seriously wrong. He had in fact mismeasured his run-up, and arrived at the crease with his right foot forward. This would have been unremarkable if he had been a left-arm bowler. He was right-handed. He tried to pull himself up but failed. He emitted a very loud scream but for all his efforts he couldn't prevent the ball from leaving his hand, from where it soared almost vertically to a great height. Everyone on the ground, including myself, rolled about with laughter. Mine however was cut short, for as the ball reached its zenith and started to descend it became clear to all that it would alight on or very near to the top of my stumps. Such was the height of the ball that I had time to think of – and discard – several ways of solving this unique problem. At first I thought of a horizontal sweep of the bat at the *moment critique*, but having been taught at school to eschew hitting across the line of the ball, I thought not. Then it occurred to me that placing the bat horizontally above the bails would afford maximum protection. This idea I discarded in the belief that if the ball did make contact with the bat it would present the wicket-keeper with a simple catch.

I therefore stood my ground, slightly bowing my head in honour of this unusual delivery. I felt a sharp tap on the nape of my neck followed by the sound of tumbling wickets.

Thus I became the only bald-headed barrister to be bowled first ball off the back of his head at the Oval.

My second claim to a world record took place in humbler surroundings. I was playing for my village, Wonersh, near Guildford. It was a typical village side, full of enthusiasm and some good natural cricketers. The spectators were as unsophisticated as the players. On one occasion I carelessly left my box on the table which was being prepared for tea. One of the wives came up to me and handed me this essential piece of equipment saying: 'Mr Tilling, I believe this is your elbow guard.' We had our fair share of eccentrics. Our number eleven was a postman of great loyalty and very decided views. If he thought he was wrongly given out he wouldn't budge. Our regular opponents soon got to know that clean bowling him was the only solution. This they had little difficulty in doing as he was a far better postman than a batsman. Though on one occasion he tried to stay put even when he had his off stump knocked out of the ground, claiming that he distinctly heard the umpire call a no-ball.

But back to my second record.

We had no ground of our own, but were lent a field by a kindly neighbouring Catholic seminary. A field in which during the week that pious institution grazed its cattle. Volunteers were called for to prepare the wicket each week. I and one other were the only members of the team who didn't work on a Saturday morning, and had the necessary implements. My friend had a mowing machine and I had a shovel. My task was to clear away all signs of the recent occupation by the cattle. Even after my efforts

the actual pitch was a little unreliable. Balls came through at varying heights and speeds according to whether they pitched where the cattle had or had not been. It completely baffled our star bowler who was a Free Forester. He never could hit the moist patches.

Once again I opened the batting. At the end of our innings I was two not out. I do not claim this to be a record, though I don't imagine it has been achieved too often. No, the record was achieved by what my ten other colleagues did – or rather didn't – do. My fellow-opener scored 1, and none the other nine scored at all. Thus my two invaluable runs were twice as many as the rest of my side put together, and this I believe can clearly never have been equalled let alone surpassed.

By the way, I've described my innings as invaluable, and so it was, for we won the match. With the help of 35 extras we beat our opponents by two runs.

SIC TRANSIT GLORIA LINDY
BOB HAWKE

As a student, represented the university of West Australia. As a Rhodes Scholar, was 12th Man for Oxford in the side captained by Colin Cowdrey, and on returning to Australia represented the Canberra area. Since becoming Prime Minister of Australia, has reinstated the annual matches between the PM's XI and touring international teams; these have become a highlight of the Canberra sporting calendar and have given up-and-coming Sheffield Shield players the opportunity to show their potential for higher honours. Next year's game against England is keenly anticipated. As well, he continues to get runs as captain of his Office XI in regular cut-throat contests against the Canberra Press Gallery.

In Australia most of December and January constitute what we know as the 'silly season', a happy time when the nation's politics like its people go on holiday and cricket drives almost everything else from public consciousness. As I write, the 1985–86 'silly season' is sadly coming to an end and, at this heavy juncture, I am led to muse on the relationship of politics and cricket.

The more obvious parallels need not be dwelt on: we all know that both are team games, in which internal dissension will inevitably hand victory to the other side; that the captaincy is an endless source of public fascination and speculation; and that the selectors are prone all too often to surprise the pundits and the players.

I am more struck by the similarities in the rhythm of politics and the traditional Test series: there are long periods of unspectacular play which are nevertheless fascinating to the informed public; much of the time one side is playing for a draw or at least seeking to consolidate after the loss of a few early wickets; and both games tend to reward those players who set themselves for the long haul, play the bowling on its merits and leave the one-day shot in the dressing-room.

Only rarely, for example during censure motions or occasionally in Question Time, is there a legitimate political parallel with the limited overs game. It is then that the slog over mid-on, the educated edge through first slip and the square cut off leg stump come into their own. On those occasions when the players and the crowd on the Hill get carried away, the Speaker has the dismissive authority of an umpire and does not need to confirm his decisions with any colleague at square leg.

Both politics and cricket have an unusual capacity to humble those who pursue them, not least in the ease and speed of the transition from fame to oblivion. Like politics, cricket provides its practitioners with a stage on which they may shine brilliantly for a time. It is given to very few, however, to live large in the public memory after their careers are over.

This is the phenomenon described by that great Australian all-rounder, Keith Miller: 'You're soon forgotten and you're a long time dead.' Or as the doyen of retired Australian Parliamentarians, Fred Daly, put it: 'You're a rooster today but a feather duster tomorrow'.

Paradoxically, the essentially fleeting medium of television may have the effect of providing an enormous archive which, properly used, will serve to keep today's cricketing greatness before the eyes of succeeding generations. In Australia at the moment, video cassettes on the history of

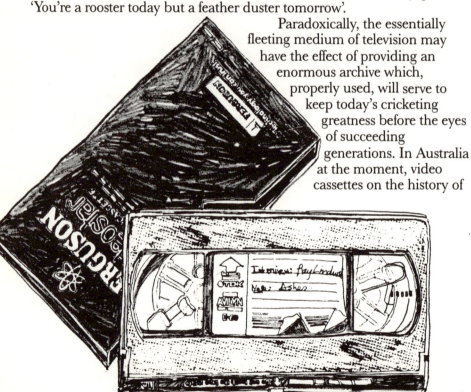

the game are growing increasingly popular. It is possible through this medium to see such master cricketers as Grace, Trumper, Hobbs, Bradman, Larwood, Grimmett and Hammond in action as well as to relive the extraordinary excitement of the tied Test at Brisbane in 1961 when Benaud, Davidson, Harvey and their colleagues took on the likes of Sobers, Kanhai and Hall. Future generations may therefore have the opportunity to witness at their leisure and in detail the style and achievements of such great contemporary cricketers as Border, Gavaskar, Gower, Hadlee, Imran and Richards.

I might add, parenthetically, that, in one respect at least, one can only be grateful that at the time much of the existing historical footage was shot, video technology was undeveloped. How would such committed appealers as 'Tiger' O'Reilly or Freddie Trueman, or such dedicated non-walkers as W.G. Grace or Bill Lawry have performed had they been able to back up their claims with the instant replay?

Whatever the future potential of television as a cricketing *aide mémoire*, I have some striking recent evidence of the easy fading of the image of even the most eminent cricketer. In the 1940s and '50s the graceful action and the great pace of Ray Lindwall were acclaimed around the world as the pinnacle of the fast bowler's art. He was the hero of Australia and the bogeyman of our opponents.

Ray last played for Australia in 1959. Since he stopped hurling down his thunderbolts and took up the more peaceful pursuit of horticulture, he has modestly eschewed the limelight.

Ray told me the other day that he had therefore been quietly surprised and gratified to be recognized as he and his wife were catching a cab home after one of this season's one-day matches. 'Aren't you Ray Lindwall?' asked the driver, his voice tinged with respect, if not awe.

Ray's brief puff of sporting pride did not last long as his questioner continued: 'The florist?'

OPENERS
FREDERIC RAPHAEL

His distinguished cricketing career, begun in wartime Sussex and developed on the fields of Charterhouse, has led him to play on some of the best beaches in the world.

Some books make us laugh so much that they should never be looked at again. Of these, for me, a prime example is Archie Macdonnell's *England Their England*. What is *Three Men In A Boat* by comparison? A tract! Macdonnell's cricket match is infinitely funnier than Dickens's in *The Pickwick Papers*, but since there is little so unforgivable, in a literary sense, as telling other people's jokes in synopsis form, I shall limit myself to recalling how, after Mr Shakespeare Pollock had made mighty contact with the bowling of the belted and braced blacksmith, he promptly dropped his bat and hared off to square leg. This hilarious aberration was due, of course, to Mr Pollock's imagining that cricket and baseball were of the same family and that his business, once a meeting had been achieved between bat and ball, was to leg it round the 'diamond' (somewhat square-cut on this occasion) before a fielder shied it at his midriff. Did he, after acculturation, prove finally adaptable to the English game or was he cruelly humbled for his misbegotten origins? Macdonnell's humour being humane, I shall continue to believe that Mr Pollock became a competent, perhaps even capped, convert to an improbable game and came at last to play a straight bat with the best, or better, of them.

I must confess to a certain kinship with Mr Pollock, since I was born within sound, if not sight, of Wrigley Field, in Chicago, where the Red Sox played and where the local newspaper was as rabidly anti-British as its proprietor, Colonel McCormack, could arrange for it to be. The mayor of my native city, Big Bill Thompson, when threatened with a visit by the King-Emperor, George V, declared that he would give His Majesty a sock in the nose, though I think that the royal progress passed off without any such bloody incident. My father was British, despite his seersucker suits and his devotion to American dance music, and he maintained an undiluted affection for cricket, even when we went to live under the shadow of Yankee Stadium, in New York. By a fluke of business politics, we had to return to London just before the war, by which time I was an unmistakable American kid, convinced that nothing in my father's country was either as big or as good as what we had in the good old US of A. My folk heroes were Babe Ruth and Jack Dempsey, a neighbour of ours on Central Park West, I would have you know. England was without names to conjure with.

In 1939, my conversion from seven-year-old Yank to eight-year-old Englishman seemed unsurprisingly swift. In retrospect, I am astonished, and even a little ashamed, at the speed of it: what kind of a leopard can change its spots so fast? The war probably put the pressure on: patriotism has small patience with half-measures and who can be more pressingly patriotic than middle-class schoolboys? If my accent conformed almost instantly, I took longer to accustom myself to the local sports. I can still recall the bewildering oddness of the cricket gear disentombed from its winter quarters in the early summer of 1940. The huge fields of my prep school were prepared for action by a tractor hauling rotating blades which appeared wider than a main road. Grass flew like green shrapnel and sweetened the Sussex air as the rumble of guns from across the Channel excited our innocent ears and made the square allotments tremble beneath our trowels as we dug for an unlikely victory.

Mr Crowe, who had the dark hair and small-eyed aspect of his corvine provenance, was deputed to teach us the elements of batting. As France tottered and fell (creating a feeling less of doom than of the happy prospect of a last-wicket stand), Mr Crowe was impatient with me: I batted the wrong way round. *Sub specie aeternitatis* (something which seemed not too remote just then), it might seem a small matter whether a beardless boy's left hand grasped the bat above or below the right. Mr Crowe, however, regarded left-handedness as akin to treason and he was in no mood to tolerate a fifth-columnist at such a juncture. Like John Donne in a more metaphysical context, I allowed prudent counsels to prevail and altered my stance.

The success of the Germans made Sussex a dangerous place for batsmen of any persuasion. In the middle of my first season, if I may put it that way, when I was beginning to 'pitch' without bending my elbow (and to fasten my pads without dislocating my shoulder), and when I had observed with fascination how Fatty Magaloon, the amiable Maths master, was transformed by copious white flannels and a Nomads sweater into someone of elegance and, as he cut and swept with unhurried flexibility, into a figure of almost balletic grace, the whole school was banished from its wide and level and vulnerable acres to the raw hills of North Devon. My headmaster's sources in the War Office had informed him that the area of Ilfracombe would be remote from enemy incursions (we saw one Heinkel, hurrying home after firing Cardiff, and a single-pronged mine which floated into the bay, causing us to rush inland, in our house shoes).

Lee Bay was garnished with a sandy beach and limpeted rocks

from which to plunge or lurch into the icy Bristol Channel, but the steepness of the protective hills was such that only a narrow playing field was available to us, at the bottom of the vee-shaped valley. A pair of bent football fields could be accommodated in it, though moles made them dangerous with inverted bunkers, but cricket was out of the question, for the duration. The hotel had tennis courts, where we became green-footed through playing without our rationed gym shoes, but the great summer game had to be postponed. Because tennis and sand-castles lacked the team element so essential to a Britannic education, a number of alternatives made brief appearances on the sporting curriculum. We played girlish rounders on the narrow field and we tried a strange game with a wooden paddle and a sort of 'wicket', for full tosses only, which consisted of a board attached to a pole. None of these soft-balled substitutes either amused or exercised us for long, but though they bore a certain similarity to what had once been my national game, no-one ever suggested that we actually play baseball. Gum- and gun-toting GIs marched through the fuschiaed villages and between the high Devon hedges, but they brought no enthusiasm for American *mores*. Looking back, I am amazed to discover in my young wartime persona not the smallest nostalgia for New York. When, in 1945, my father refused to return to the USA, saying that he had committed me to an English education, I took it as the final signal to embrace all things British. During that last summer of prep school, we returned to Sussex: the great rotating blades resumed their tonsile task and the greening pads were taken from under the latticed benches of the pavilion and blancoed for the resumption of peacetime conflict. The war was over.

The following autumn, I was sent to Charterhouse. My only link with it was that Fatty Magaloon had been a Nomad, which meant, more or less, that he had been in the fourth eleven. It seemed, and remains, an unattainable eminence. It had qualified him for a richly embroidered sweater (or 'hasher', as I had to learn to call it) and made him the lowest form of 'blood'. In the hope that I might emulate him, my father sent me to Alf Gover's indoor school during the Easter holidays. Some of the Surrey professionals used to hang out there, occasionally turning over their arms and rattling the stumps (set in a wooden block) of some cocksure pupil. I enjoyed their insiders' dialogue and envied their ability to smoke and bowl tweakers at the same time. After a few sessions with bat and ball, I looked forward to school cricket with some enthusiasm. Big Alf said that I ought to do well. I was given a new pair of boots, with impressive studs, and a Walter Hammond autograph bat. Ready when you are, W.G.

I was somewhat dashed to be put in Lockites' 'Second Tics' for my first game; there was no lower category. I had hoped that our house captain might at least put me in 'Yearlings', which contained the pick of the new boys, but my uncultivated football, during the winter terms, must have disillusioned him. When, in the first match, I scored twenty-five not out, in a total of about sixty, I had reason to think I might be promoted. My father had warned me on no account to be pushy, so I accepted my steady omission until half term. Then, one day, I came upon the house captain, who went under the sumptuous name of Brough Stuart Churchill Gurney Randall, a dead ringer for Harold Nicolson's J.D. Marstock in *Some People*, just as he was actually writing out the team sheets. As his pen hesitated (he probably couldn't think of an eleventh Yearling), I murmured that I found Second Tics a little boring and rather wished that, before the year was out, I might have a chance in Yearlings. He scrawled my name on the list at once.

It was not only the season when Compton and Edrich made 'statistics' into a term redolent of glory (I was a Middlesex supporter, despite Alf Gover and his wristy friends), it was also a summer when P.B.H. May (Saunderites) scored a century in every home match that

Charterhouse played. The resident professional, Leicestershire and England's George Geary, is said to have told the young maestro, when he was fifteen, that there was nothing more he could teach him. It was indeed difficult to imagine what could be missing from May's game; he turned cricket into a form of one-man show. When he played in house matches, scoring as many runs as were needed to enable him to bowl out the opposition in the name of Saunderites, it was as if an Olympian had deigned to play skittles with mortals. Peter was blessed with one great gift beyond that of being a virtuoso: he was modest to a fault. He dreaded flattery and eschewed arrogance. In a school vicious with vanity and charmless with charlatans, May was the perfect sportsman. It is perhaps a small pity that, with his boundless skills, he never looked very happy. If he had been a bully and a braggart and a bastard, what a time he would have had!

As the years went by, I continued to attend Alf Gover's nursery and as I grew taller and stronger, the genial demon kindly assured me that I should soon be in the school eleven. In fact, even in my last year, I got no further than our house team. I might not be a bad bowler in the nets, but nerves led me to serve up long-hops and full tosses in a match. Since we had two arrow-fast Scots, who needed only very short rests before resuming their accurate intimidations, I was rarely thrown the ball. Frankly, as long as I was in the side, I hardly cared. I was a good slip fielder and I became a reliable batsman of the most constipated rectitude. My finest hour came in a house match against Gownboys, who paraded a 1st XI left-arm bowler called Holt. Berkeley, our house captain (we were not on first-name terms after four years of proximity), asked me to go in number one, which he did not seem to regard as a privilege, more a form of sacrifice. Thinking of Robertson and Sailor Brown, who broke the fast men of other counties so that Edrich W.J. and Compton D.C.S. might then carve them to the four corners of Lord's, I elected to be flattered.

If I say so myself, I never played better. After an hour and a half, I was still there. After an hour and forty minutes, I had only just been dismissed. It is true that I had made only seventeen runs, which may not seem much of a highlight to those who have smug averages, but it was – and the symbolism is crucial – precisely the same number of runs that Edrich W.J. had scored in the first Test match in Australia after the war. I had heard the crackling, wheezing, coming-and-going story of his epic knock against bouncers and steak-fed beamers in the early morning of a savagely cold English winter and I shall never forget the commentator (was it Rex Alston?) saying that in cricket what mattered was not how many runs you scored, but how you scored them. Sir Henry Newbolt might not have put it better, what? And so, when I came off the field after exhausting Holt by the unspeakable unadventurousness of my forward defensive shot, I did not see my comatose team-mates but rather a jury of bearded immortals who, with their grave applause, acknowledged that, for certain purposes, I could indeed pass for an Englishman, at last.

We lost the game in the end, though not before I had held a flashing slip catch when the scores were level (the batsman was caught literally red-handed, the hands being mine). Truly, on that day I could do little wrong. (Our skipper gave me no opportunity for long-hops: Nichols and Buchan-Hepburn bowled right through the Gownboy innings, until some spoil-sport nicked their winning run.) I do not wish to darken the light-hearted tone of this memoir, so I will not dwell on the loathing I felt, and feel, for Charterhouse. It is enough to say, with characteristic understatement, that it was a school for fools and fascists. However, that night it provided me with one of the happiest moments of my life.

Colours were called 'House Teams' and to be awarded them was to 'receive House Teams'. The house captain drawing-pinned a card on the notice board with the favoured names on it. I might be blasé about scholarships, but I hardly dared to look when Berkeley thumbed his few nominations onto the green baize. I had never been popular and I expected no palsy preferment. I glanced as casually as I could at the board. 'After the match against Gownboys,' I read, 'F.M. Raphael received House Teams.' I might never be a Nomad, with an enviable hasher, but I was now entitled to wear an apple-green and black striped neckerchief. It is the only pleasure that damned school ever gave me. When, in our last match of the season, I was given out, caught at the wicket by Burton-Brown, after padding a ball well outside the off stump, with my bat high in the air, my American blood made me want to fling down my bat and run, not to square leg but all the way to Southampton. However, the British graft had conclusively taken: flannelled fool, I thought of P.B.H. May and, with a look worthy of Sydney Carton's understudy, I quit the field, never to return, cursing the blind umpire and looking for all the world like the next best thing to a gentleman.

CAUGHT THREE WAYS
MIKE SEABROOK

Gave up playing because of total incompetence. Now umpires with the Middlesex League, based at Ealing CC.

It was very early in my career as a cricketer that I revealed with devastating clarity that I lacked every single one of the qualities needed to make a good player – or even one of passable mediocrity. Because I loved the game passionately, I looked for something that I could do on the cricket field with some semblance of ability, and quickly found my niche in umpiring. It was as regular umpire for my University XI that I took part in an epic encounter one deep, sultry summer. As such, I think I was very lucky to be a part of this match. This was because it was one of those games in which the laws of cricket are pretty well at a discount and there would hardly seem to be any need for umpires at all. Games in which the best way might well be, as Roy Kilner once said of Roses matches, 'no umpires and fair cheating all round'.

The University XI had been let down by some team, and a substitute fixture was arranged at short notice. The game took place in a tiny hamlet on the coast. The cricket field belonged to a local farmer of indecent wealth, and the teams changed in his splendid house and walked to the ground along a deep grass lane. The banks reared up twelve feet on either side, topped by trees whose heavy canopies of leaves met overhead, so that walking down the steep lane was like walking in a kind submarine twilight, or through the nave of a cool green-lit cathedral.

The ground itself ran down to a tall cliff, and the game was played to a perpetual accompaniment of the soothing murmur of Atlantic breakers on the beach far below and the cries of gulls and terns. The pitch was on a gradient of about one in ten, and it was perilous to chase too hard towards the square-leg boundary, for the ground fell away sharply towards the edge of the cliff, crumbling dramatically at the brink; and there was no fence or anything else to stop a fielder whose brakes failed from plunging straight over the edge.

The wicket was mown and rolled after a fashion, but the outfield was shaggy and redolent of grasses and flowers. The wind was fierce at all times and a tempest at the drop of a hat. The sky was a perpetual armada

52

of clouds racing across the sky, and the fielders near the cliff were cooled by occasional lashes of spray from below. The other three boundaries were fringed with nodding apple boughs. The pavilion was a potting shed, with sacks and cobwebs and tools.

Our side started the match in the field. I was fortunate enough to have no appeals early on. If I had I might have made the error of giving someone out. As it was, nothing came my way before I had had a chance to size up the situation and decide that I was going to allow nature to take its course that day.

Ten minutes after we started the first of the village batsmen was bowled neck and crop. As he walked off to the potting shed he called, in a thick rural burr: 'Arry! Ere, Arry! Bring er oat!' At this, Arry emerged from the shed bearing a large earthenware jug and a kind of ladle shaped like a mug on a stick. This he then carried out to the middle. The two batsmen, along with the one who had just got out, made bee-lines for him, and the rest of us followed curiously.

In the great jug was a livid greenish fluid. It had things like big yellow polyps, or gobs of phlegm, floating in it, and it smelled alarmingly. Arry dipped the ladle-mug and handed it to the nearest player, who drank deeply – the ladle was about three-quarters of a pint. Then it passed round the rest of us. The evil-looking potion was amazingly cool and good. You felt refreshed immediately. It was one of the local brews of rough cider, otherwise scrumpy. We all drank the commercial stuff, but none of us had ever tasted one like this. We drank eagerly. 'Plenny more whirr that come from,' we were assured. And there was. We had some more, ten minutes later, when the next wicket fell. And some more, eight minutes later, when the third one fell. And so on through an innings in which the intervals between wickets became shorter every time. The last batsman never appeared at all. He was later found in the longest grass under the apple boughs, sleeping peacefully and snoring like an old bull terrier.

The village had mustered about fifty runs, and it was our turn to bat. Our opening batsmen were both minor county prospects. The better of the two weaved his way to the receiver's end, took guard, looked blearily round, faced an atrocious full toss, whirled his very expensive bat like a flail at it, missed by several feet and was bowled. He then weaved his way back and went to sleep. On his way back he was passed by the camp follower, Arry, 'bringin er oat'. The team of university and minor county cracks had mustered thirty-one for nine, watched by me, swaying and blinking like an owl on a branch in a storm, when the captain came to the wicket. He was a very large man, of prodigious girth, but with almost freakishly tiny arms, like a barrel equipped with penguin's flippers, thick round glasses and a permanent sunny grin.

He rolled to the wicket, like a barrel breasting its way through a strong tide, the bat looking like a toy. He folded himself up like a penknife in order to ground the bat in the crease, and smote the first ball he received (another atrocious full toss) a mile high and half a mile out to sea. So, at least, it seemed to me, watching yet more owlishly under the influence of several more ladles of the green fluid, getting thicker as we proceeded down the immense vessel we had seen in Arry's shed.

Several fielders started clambering down the cliff, but were soon glad to give up such a suicidal mission. We then had to find a spare ball. After a great deal of standing on heads in the shed we all emerged, coughing and spluttering, covered in tickly dust and wreathed in huge nets of cobwebs, the blackness and stickiness of which seemed to have been quite unaffected by their antiquity, with a disreputable, misshapen and faded object that had once been a gleaming fat cricket ball. It was almost literally falling to pieces, and had an impressive fringe of white beard protruding through the seam all round the girth.

After our exertions in the shed we needed a couple of draughts of the green liquid to steel us for the last leg of the homeric match. Eventually, however, we managed to persuade eight or nine fielders and the two batsmen to stagger out to the wicket again, accompanied by myself to umpire at both ends should the need arise.

It didn't. Ken, our captain, was to receive only one more ball. The shaggy, filthy ball came twirling and humming through the air at him (another full toss), and he launched another of his enormous heaves at it. It was a rare occasion when Ken managed to make contact with a ball; but this one he did hit, with all his eighteen stone behind it. It met his bat with a sort of soggy 'splat!', and flew high in the air in a curvetting flight as the wind caught in the beard. As it rose it also finally gave up the ghost, and flew apart in three directions, like a black, solid roman candle. The match was now over, for there certainly was no other ball, and we were in no state to seek it if there had been. In any case, it was finally agreed, after much discussion round the cider vat, that Ken had been dismissed: caught at first slip, fine leg and deepish extra cover. I was consulted on this as the official in charge of the game. Deciding that it would be unfair to deny three worthy efforts – for anybody to have had sufficient presence of mind left to catch anything at all was no mean achievement that day – I raised an unsteady finger, and we all went off to the village pub for a much-needed drink.

BRAMALL LANE MEMORIES
ROY HATTERSLEY

Has been a member of the Yorkshire County Cricket Club for forty years. He was captain of cricket at the Sheffield City Grammar School and during his first year at Hull University played, occasionally, for the 1st XI and regularly for the 2nd.

On summer Saturdays back in 1950, the pavilion at Bramall Lane was packed from boundary to balcony when Yorkshire were playing in Sheffield. Eager county members, anxious for a seat behind the bowler's arm, brought in their sandwiches and vacuum flasks two hours before play began and – having staked their claim to a specific piece of splintering wooden bench – walked off to the nets to wait for their heroes to begin the morning's loosening up.

In those halcyon days (days in which I learned the meaning of 'halcyon' from the collected works of Neville Cardus) I arrived at the pavilion entrance at about one o'clock and left again at the beginning of the lunch interval half an hour later. For in the morning I played for the Sheffield City Grammar School in a twenty-over-a-side competition which marked the beginning of my hatred for the limited-overs game. And in the afternoon I tried to bat properly for Wadsley Church or the YMCA. In between the two failures, which typified my usual Saturday, I squeezed in thirty minutes at Bramall Lane. Never in the pavilion itself, because the pavilion was full. But round behind third man where the bowling was from the end variously described as the brewery, the football stand or St Mary's – depending on whether the commentator's tastes were alcoholic, all-round sporting or ecclesiastical.

I hated sitting in the little pavilion annexe. The scoreboard was behind me, the slips obscured my view of the batsman, when strike was at my end, and, worst of all, Len Hutton was unlikely to score any boundaries in my direction. Len Hutton played his shots to the off in front of the wicket. He late cut rarely, on-drove (at least for four) only infrequently and snicked through the slips never. And I went to Bramall Lane to see Len Hutton bat. I still think of the ground and the batsman as

56

being inseparable. No doubt he preferred playing nearer to home at
Headingley. Indeed, I have heard him speak of his days as Yorkshire's
senior apprentice – carrying George Hirst's cricket bat to the Leeds tram
stop – with an undisguised sentimentality about that ground and its
famous slope. And if the Oval was not his favourite pitch, it certainly
should have been. But I think of him as driving into the covers at Bramall
Lane.

In almost two decades of cricket passion, I only saw a handful of
full days' play on that ground. On match days I was at school, at work or
playing on the sloping pitches of the Pennine foothills where the batting
squares were cut into the hillsides and fielders on the lower boundary
stood with their heads at about the same height as the batsman's boots. It
was whilst watching such a game during the war that my father told me
that the outfield at Bramall Lane was flatter, better kept and more closely
cut than the wickets on Wadsley Common.

In the 1940s, little boys did not run on to the pitch. But one day –
I think it was in 1949 – I arrived at the Lane so early that I was able to

tiptoe out through the gap in the fence which was left open for the arrival of the heavy roller. It was true. I had never actually seen a billiard table because billiard halls were thought, by my parents, to encourage vice as successfully as cricket promoted virtue. But the outfield was as I imagined a billiard table to be. I felt sure that if only I took guard on a batting strip as flat as that I would begin to score runs.

The early-morning exploration, back in 1949, ended in disaster and disgrace. For it took place on a Wednesday – a day when I should have been at school. Because of the necessity to leave home as usual at eight o'clock I arrived outside the great pavilion gates before the groundsman had opened them. I can remember almost everything about that day. Before play began I watched the brewery chimney above and beyond the football stand, hoping that just for once it would puff out the sort of black smoke with which, legend claimed, it always darkened the skies when Lancashire were batting on a Bank Holiday Monday. And I infuriated an old codger, who rashly sat next to me for a moment, by reading the *Daily Telegraph* crossword in his lap and telling him that 'nimble like the navy' meant 'fleet'. I must have been inspired by my surroundings. For I had never before – nor have I ever since – felt any attraction or possessed any talent for crossword puzzles.

Unfortunately the Yorkshire team were not similarly possessed. 'Roly' Jenkins bowled in his cap. Cooper and Kenyon scored a large number of runs. Yorkshire lost to Worcestershire for the first time in the history of the County Championship. The consolation of Len Hutton carrying his bat through the Yorkshire innings was spoilt when, running home, I literally bumped into Miss Waddington, the City Grammar's zoology mistress, who had popped into the ground after school to enjoy the last two hours of play. I still forged the letter about being in bed with a heavy cold. But even as I tried to reproduce my mother's signature, I knew that the game was lost.

I was prohibited from playing cricket for the school for the rest of the season. So having, at last, emerged from the second eleven, I was to miss two Saturday games (when there was not even a match to watch at Bramall Lane in the morning) and the School versus Staff fixture on the last day of term. School versus Staff was not important, even though it was the one game at which we could perform in front of spectators when the whole school was shipped off to the playing field to watch the annual event. The match against Woodhouse Grammar School was, on the other hand, crucial. For Hodgson and Bilham opened the bowling for Woodhouse and Hodgson and Bilham were Yorkshire Colts. A part of me was relieved to miss the challenge. But most of me wanted to see, to try, to judge – just for once.

The consolation came in August. By some luck of the draw or irrationality of fate, the youth team of the Wadsley Church Cricket Club (an institution which had no more connection with the Wadsley Parish than Southampton Football Club has with St Mary's) survived long enough in the Norton and District knock-out league to be drawn against Sheffield United. Again the opening bowlers were well known to me. Oakes and Cottrell – as well as playing for Sheffield United's senior side in the Yorkshire Council – were colleagues in the City Grammar School team. Well, colleagues of a sort…As they explained at school, on the day of the match, their senior status required them to play in only a proportion of the junior games; but, when they had heard that I was batting first wicket down for that evening's opponents, they had decided that they 'would be daft' not to turn out. What did it matter, I thought. None of their instincts could deny me the prize. I was going to bat at Bramall Lane.

And so I did. Both teams changed in the visitors' dressing room. So it was not until another thirty years had passed that I managed to stand on the Yorkshire balcony – and only then whilst making a recording for a television film which marked the pavilion's demolition. But on an evening – back in 1949 – I looked through Bramall Lane Pavilion glass to the pitch which I would soon occupy. The wicket was pitched twenty yards to the left of where the stumps would be set for a county match. But I knew that the outfield was flatter than the squares on which I usually batted, so that did not worry me. What did was the sight of my parents sitting in absolute isolation, in the pavilion annexe underneath the scoreboard. There was not another spectator on the ground. I decided to brazen it through. With any luck, nobody would know that they belonged to me.

United won the toss and, as was usual in those matches, elected to field. Our opening batsman, one Brian Stephenson who was known as 'Chloe' for reasons wholly unconnected with Debussy, was out first ball. So I was, virtually, opening the batting where I had seen my hero, Len Hutton, open it so many times before. I walked to the wicket touching the peak of my scarlet City Grammar School cap in the way that HE touched the peak of his blue Yorkshire cap. I tried not to look at my parents and not to be unnerved by the Sheffield United umpire who was also their coach and, after giving me my middle and leg guard in his first capacity then, acting in his second, advised Derek Cottrell to reinforce his slips. If my appearance at Bramall Lane had been a decent adventure story, I would have made either a duck (as a penalty for the rejection of my parents) or enough runs to secure victory over the arrogant fast bowlers. In fact I pushed and prodded a dozen and walked back up the pavilion steps imagining the members had stood up to applaud me home.

I have heard and seen plenty of applause at Bramall Lane. I watched Ted Lester – now the Yorkshire scorer – catch Everton Weekes on the long-leg boundary in both innings of one match. I saw Keith Miller drop a sitter at second slip and Don Bradman pick up the ball and press it into Miller's hand as if he were returning a rattle that had fallen out of a baby's pram. I saw Don Brennan stump Martin Donnelly when the New Zealander went down the wicket to 'garden' – believing that the ball was dead. I saw Walter Hammond score a century in the 'Victory Test' against the Australian Imperial Forces, Denis Compton bitten by a stray dog, and Fred Trueman carried off with a ruptured muscle in his back. And I saw Len Hutton and Frank Lawson flay the South African attack whilst Eric Rowan, fielding on the boundary's edge, told the spectators that neither of them was any good.

It now seems extraordinary that all of what was once the cricket ground has now been swept away. Or nearly all. The scoreboard has gone. But the pavilion annexe in front of it has somehow escaped the bulldozer. From the new football stand – its front-row seats taking up about the position at which the slips once stood – survivors from the Forties and Fifties can recognize the one remaining feature of the good old days. I was there in the stand last December. And as I looked down on the archaeological remains I still felt the embarrassment of seeing my parents sitting there during my single Bramall Lane innings, and annoyance that I used to be squeezed into the part of the ground where my hero, Len Hutton, never scored any of his immaculate boundaries.

GENTLEMEN AND PLAYERS

JOHN EBDON

In addition to the rich playing career outlined in his essay, he claims not to have missed a single Test commentary since 1947, and except for five years spent in Kenya never to have been absent from the first day's play of a Lord's Test. All this dedication seems to have paid off, for he has recently been invited to become a Lord's Taverner.

Cricket is as English as roast beef, as permanent as poverty, and as unpredictable as present Anglican theology. It is my second religion. I genuflect when passing the Marylebone Cricket Club, bow my head at the name of Wisden and pine during the winter months when the game goes into hibernation, longing for the moment when football hooligans put away their flick-knives and when once again the air is filled with the sweet sound of willow on leather (and occasionally leather on bone) and the unforgettable smells of drying pitches and drying flannels as summer arrives with its customary wetness. Moreover, I always associate the game with my father.

A simple man, his philosophy of life was refreshingly uncomplicated. Either one 'played the game' or one did not. Those who kept to the rules were gentlemen, regardless of their social status, and those who ignored them were bounders. Or worse. To those categories were admitted men who displayed coloured propelling pencils or fountain pens in their top pockets, and those who sported club ties to which they were not entitled. Equally beyond the pale were those who gave tongue at Twickenham when conversions were being attempted or who left their seats during overs at Lord's. Such things were 'not done', which is why I am glad my father is no longer with us for nowadays they are; and sport is the poorer for both gestures.

My father was a splendid mentor. He taught me how to gather and pass a rugby ball when I was seven, advised me that only soccer players or dagos made a fuss when they were kicked, and at the same age instructed me how to hold a cricket bat. He applauded me roundly when I broke two scullery windows in quick succession off his under-arm deliveries with a soft ball, mollified our general factotum who was working at the sink at the time by bribing her with a shilling; and by spanking me soundly for kicking my wicket in a fit of pique when he had adjudged me lbw, he instilled in me the importance of accepting an umpire's decision at all times, and of being a good loser. As I was seldom allowed the luxury of being a good winner, this advice was to prove invaluable to me in life.

Despite the early promise I displayed in our back garden, I never excelled as a batsman. True, I once made eighty-six for a scratch eleven in Colombo whilst batting against an equally bizarre opposition fielding among other Singalese notables a drunken first slip and a cross-eyed fast bowler with a suspect action and a crab-like approach, but it was a transitory moment of glory never to be repeated; and I regretted that my father was not present to savour the performance. Had he been able so to do, his life would have been enriched immeasurably. Furthermore, he would have been given hope that I was destined to emulate the feats of my forebears: I had three great uncles who played a total of ten innings for Somerset. One of them, Jack Ebdon, scored two runs at Taunton and then wisely and fulsomely devoted himself to the study of mediaeval French. As it was, fate ordained that my father should watch me being bowled round my legs for three when playing in a Fathers v Sons match at my progeny's preparatory school in Berkshire. Shortly afterwards he was further humiliated when, dressed in a pair of E. R. Dexter's flannels loaned to me by Madame Tusssaud's, who had used them to clothe a waxen facsimile of the great man, I skidded on the damp turf near the boundary, totally destroying a deckchair and drawing blood from its occupant accoutred in a panama hat and an MCC tie. Like Queen Victoria, he was not amused. The dramaturgy provoked huzzahs and cheers from all but the ensanguined incumbent who wished me to perdition with a rare turn of phrase, my son who was deeply embarrassed by the spectacle; and my father. It was not a happy day for him. However, he hid his disappointment bravely.

'After all,' said he, his voice vibrant with insincerity, 'it doesn't matter that you made a fool of yourself. After all,' he repeated, 'it's only a game.' My son who had been keeping wicket and whom I had caught at mid-on with his half-century in sight, said nothing. Nor has he ever referred to that chapter in our family history. Enthusiastic agnostic though he be, my son is a fine exponent of Christian charity. On the other hand my father, who was a devout churchman, did allude to it. Frequently.

Although unlike the late General Montgomery, my father never spoke of his Maker as 'that Great Umpire in the Sky' or prayed that he be allowed to 'hit the enemy for six', much of his vocabulary was made up of sporting metaphors. Shortly before he died, unpleasantly but with a quiet dignity from cancer in a Cottage Hospital, I visited him and looked with sadness at the yellowing echo of the man who had taken me to Lord's for the first time. His eyes were still blue but rheumy with age and illness and a copy of *In Defence of the Ashes* lay opened and face down on the coverlet.

I stayed for a while, talking quietly in a desultory fashion about trivialities until he closed his eyes and dozed, and in his half sleep returned to the Somme and Flanders fields and mumbled the name of his younger brother, who had fallen as others had done, in bloody heaps at Menin. And he called upon his father and the King and cried out for stretcher bearers; and spoke the names of Larwood and Hutton and Chamberlain and Hendren. And so I waited with him as the spectres of half a century flitted through his muddled mind.

It was when I disengaged my hand from his and eased myself from the bed that he re-awakened. I said: 'I think it's time I went now. But I'll see you tomorrow, if that's all right?'

The blue eyes looked hazily but directly at me under half-lowered lids. 'Yes', he said, 'Yes. Of course. But I think it's time I was getting back to the pavilion too'. He gave a little sigh like that of a tired child at the end of a long day. 'After all', he said, 'I've been at the crease for quite a while you know…quite a while…I've had a very good innings'. And gently turning his head away, he smiled into the pillow.

Later that evening I was told that he had died and for a long while I mourned his passing, for with his death, or so it seemed to me, a little Englishness had been lost and a little greenness had gone from the land. But I was wrong. My father's generation may be clay but others have taken their place. And with the ghosts of yesteryear they sit in the great cricket grounds around the country, as essential to the scene as the young men in white in the middle.

Politely they applaud a glance to the leg; gently they murmur their approval of a well set field; and cumbersomely, but as one man, they rise to give an ovation to a century maker. Occasionally, usually after luncheon, their chins telescope, tortoise-like toward their chests and their faces show pink beneath their hats, and they perspire. But like my father and his contemporaries, they never, ever leave their seats during overs.

THE ART OF BEING CAPTAINED

PETER GIBBS

Was a first-class cricketer with Oxford University and Derbyshire from 1964-72. As an opening batsman he made nearly 9,000 runs including 12 centuries. Since then he has been a writer of plays for radio, television and the stage. Two of his television pieces, Arthur's Hallowed Ground, a film for David Puttnam's 'First Love' series on Channel 4, and Benefit of the Doubt on BBC 2, which won the Radio Times television script prize, had cricketing backgrounds.

Have you noticed how often cricket books contain a chapter on captaincy? Whole books are given up to all that strategy nonsense, yet nowhere will you find a chapter entitled 'The Art of Being Captained'. On the face of it this is a surprising omission since there are ten of us to one of them, but then cricket always was a bosses' game.

The chapter I have in mind would include advice on how a bowler gets to bowl at the best end; how to slip down the batting order when the wicket's a shade too green; and how to drop catches off the captain's bowling and still stay in the team. Nobody could doubt that these skills have more relevance to a cricketer's enjoyment of the game than rolling the wrists or bracing the left leg into the delivery stride.

True, most coaching manuals suggest that players should keep an eye on the captain, but only because he may want to change a fielder's position in the outfield. This is an extremely naive notion since a fielder will often pick his position with singular care – close to a hospitality tent for example or a pretty face, or away from that patch of the outfield plagued with ridges, craters and broken teeth. In such cases keep an eye on the captain by all means but first make sure that you don't catch his. Recommended is a head-bowed, eye-cocked position. Using this method (a cap helps) an outfielder can observe the captain trying to attract his attention. At first the captain will use the grand arm's-length semaphore, then the vexed handclap, finally the short crude gesticulation. A captain so trained will soon give up and start fiddling with someone else, leaving the outfielder to patrol his chosen terrain in peace.

Once mastered, the technique of getting into the captain's blind spot is extremely useful – when he's looking for a nightwatchman for example, or someone to bowl with a wet ball. One of the most common applications is sidling unnoticed away from catching positions. Sidling has a huge membership. For a close-to-the-wicket fielder this means standing so that the ball always bounces safely in front of him. On the boundary edge the sidling fielder is the one who hates waiting underneath a catch. When a batsman comes in who favours the rustic heave-ho to the legside, the fielder will ignore the captain and sidle towards the sight screen. By doing this he ensures that instead of the skier straight into and possibly out of his lap, he has to gallop desperately round the boundary – whereupon he will either pluck a catch out of thin air to the surprise and plaudits of spectators or invite their sympathy for a gallant effort made in vain.

A chapter entitled 'The Art of Being Captained' would also tackle the sinister practice of brainwashing. For example, unless a player is very careful, a captain may seek to 'get the best out of him'. Now there are days, frankly, when a chap doesn't want someone getting the best out of him. Of course, he could bowl batsmen out and score runs if he wanted to, but sometimes he just prefers to be left alone to have a good sulk.

The captain trying to get the best out of a player can be spotted in a number of ways. If he approaches a bowler pretending to get some shine onto a very old ball, the bowler should move in the opposite direction, ideally with a limp. The key word to listen for here is 'brake', as in 'Just put a brake on the run rate, old son.'

Batting with the captain can be a particular minefield. Watch out for the observation from his end that you appear to have the measure of the raw West Indian quickie who is enthusiastically discolouring your torso by numbers. The giveaway word here is 'middle', as in 'Your bat seems all middle today, so I'll stay down this end while you see him off.'

Players should beware of such appeals to their self-esteem and recognize that the captain himself may be vulnerable on that flank. If, after a mix-up when running between the wickets, a batsman finds the captain standing alongside, he should suggest that the PR value in him 'walking' would far outweigh the cost of his wicket.

Admittedly such a ploy never worked for me, but then I came from a hard-bitten North Midlands tradition where the captains tended less to the Brearleyan persuasion and more towards the 'do it or else' school of thought.

My first captain had a face as rough as a coalminer's kneepad and he could spit a lot further than some of the England team. These were invaluable assets for leading a junior school side and he was a great success until the teacher discovered that every time a coin was tossed he demanded the money with menaces.

Much as I would have enjoyed a reputation for being 'difficult' to handle, the opportunity never really presented itself. After my first hundred in league cricket the captain responded to my triumphant return to the dressing room with the greeting: 'If you die tonight, we'll manage.' I think he must have been the father of my junior school captain. Anyone who spoke his mind in that team spoke it in the privacy of the pavilion's outside loo. Nobody ever challenged the captain's right to play sheet anchor in a run chase and he never went on holiday for fear of a coup. Irrespective of the state of the wicket, if he won the toss he always put the opposition in to bat so that our batsmen could get their eyes used to the light. In every match he bowled the same two seam bowlers for ninety minutes whether they were getting wickets or a whopping. The spinners would then come on for fifteen minutes whereupon the seamers would return. The captain's mind ran so often down the same track we called him ASLEF.

In many ways playing under ASLEF was the best possible grounding for the first-class game. Here the captain presides over a team living together as a 'family' with all the mutual recrimination and lack of communication implied by that term. The non-stop first-class diet of cricket, travel and hotels means that the art of being captained extends beyond the cricket ground and into every waking moment.

During the evenings away from home the captain will tend to be either a nanny or a nighthawk. The nanny sits with notepad and pencil in the hotel bar after ten thirty, wearing a dressing gown and pyjamas. The nighthawk is the one who wakes a player at two in the morning to tell him it's his turn to be chauffeur.

In the morning the captain can be categorized as a dosser or a sunbeam. A dosser is so monosyllabic and lifeless at breakfast that uncapped members of the team are rostered to help him take the top off his egg. A sunbeam is the one who asks players to go to the ground with him three hours early in order to inspect the wicket. He particularly enjoys crawling under the covers to accomplish this task. Players can avoid all these types by booking into a different hotel.

In essence, then, the art of being captained is a variation on the time-honoured technique of keeping oneself scarce. Always remember, if you go looking for advice the chances are you'll get some. So, to recap, on the field of play remember to stand with the weight nicely balanced between both feet, the body alert but relaxed, arms free to move at all times, head still, keep your eye on the captain and above all keep moving. Oh, and don't forget to limp.

PUT NOT YOUR TRUST IN PRINCES
MAHARAJA OF BARODA

Born with a diamond-studded platinum spoon in his right hand and a cricket bat carved from a palm tree in his left, he began playing the game as soon as he could walk. The wicket was chalked on one of the palace walls. In 1946-47, at the age of sixteen, he made his first-class début. Once, when Vijay Hazare and Gul Mahomed were establishing their world record partnership of 577 for any first-class wicket, for Baroda v Holkar, he was the next man in and had to wait nearly three days to get a bat. He thinks this is also a world record.

For the purpose of this historical, and at times rather hysterical, article, it would be irrelevant either to probe into the origins of cricket or delve into its bulky historical records. Cricket 'came, saw and conquered' wherever the tentacles of the 'nation of shopkeepers' could extend and maintain its firm grip over a given period of time. The end of the Second World War saw the beginning of the decline and fall of that mighty and glittering Empire, its remnants now better known by its lack-lustre and ordinary name, 'The Commonwealth'. Within the walls of this crumbling citadel, once known as the British Empire, an 'Empire on which', it was justly claimed, 'the sun never set', but on which now the sun never rises, two great British gifts still flourish and precariously hold together a mysterious bond between the one-time conqueror and the conquered – the English language and the great game of cricket.

Over the years, both have withstood the devastation of time. Very artfully and tactfully they have fought and won the battle for survival, by accepting the fact that the only way to achieve this was to adapt and not confront. While the English language has enriched itself by accepting words and expressions from almost all languages, the game of cricket is flourishing by its adoption of different brands in different countries to suit the dynamic characteristics of race, religion, colour, temperament, etc.

The annals of the game pay silent tribute to the diverse contributions made to the sport by all cricket-playing countries. However, the most unusual, the most romantic and perhaps the most fascinating chapters have been provided by 'The Jewel in the Crown'.

While the Australians were building up their cricket in the outback, the South Africans in the bush and the West Indians on their sunny sands to the rhythm of the calypso, the people of the sub-continent of India did it the only way they knew.

A cricket match was a festive occasion only to be surpassed by Royal Ascot. The white sahibs turned up immaculately attired in multi-coloured blazers, and white flannels held in place by the old school tie. The memsahibs dressed up as if they were en route to a Garden Party at Buckingham Palace, and the native women came dressed and bejewelled as if going to a marriage. All around the perimeter of the ground stood colourful and stately marquees, their floors covered by the most fabulous Persian rugs. Throughout the day liveried servants catered for all the whims that pomp and opulence demanded. A Regimental band played before the commencement of the game, during lunch hour, and after the match. Lunch was a two-hour affair – the first hour and a half for champagne, chilled beer or pink gins, and half an hour for food. Those who had to make runs made them amidst thunderous applause. There were never any complaints about poor umpiring, except from the odd 'unsporting' type. A gangling, freckled lieutenant was happy to be back in the pavilion where the Colonel's cuddly daughter and a chilled beer awaited him.

In the very early stages, the British in India played a bit of club or village cricket when they felt a little homesick. Later, some 'natives', or 'brown Englishmen', just home from Eton and Harrow, Oxford and Cambridge, whose English accent was strange and whose habits too hedonistic and repulsive to some of the great religions practised in India, joined in because they felt they were superior to their own brethren, and inferior to their conquerors.

While the conqueror and the conquered were playing club cricket, about 5,000 miles away a dusky Eastern potentate was making cricketing history on English soil. In only a few summers 'Ranji' became a household word. For the first time, the British realized that Indian magic was more than just the oft-abused rope trick, that muscle power and sheer brute strength were nothing compared to the poetry that emanated from a lithe brown body, possessing steely yet pliable wrists, eagle-eyed and equipped with feet whose nimbleness would have put a Pavlova to shame.

A delectable deflection to fine leg was named the 'Ranji' glance in appreciation and acknowledgment of class.

Ranjitsinghji's exploits were soon the most talked of subject right from Viceregal circles down to clubs and Regimental Messes. Animated discussions in powder rooms were held to decide who of the recent arrivals from Home possessed the best Ranji glance. Each had a different definition for a 'glance', but in the ultimate analysis it was the best-looking young man who got the vote. However, by far the greatest and most electrifying effects of the Indian Prince's prowess were felt in the Indian Native States, where the discussion stage was quickly left behind and replaced by concrete plans, which in turn were soon transformed into action.

The result was staggering. The traditional rivals among the Rulers of Indian States saw in this an opportunity to gain superiority where they had failed in becoming more prosperous than a rival or in acquiring higher titles from the British. A vast recruitment drive was soon on the way. Talented Indian players were pressed into service, and if that was not enough, overseas players from Australia and England were bought. Soon some native States were fielding their own sides. The crafty British were quick to grab this heaven-sent opportunity of further weaning away the Ruler from his State and his people, thus enabling the British Resident to become more powerful and influential.

By the year 1930 the Princes were dominating the scene of Indian cricket, and particularly its politics. An unofficial Indian team visited England, and thereafter official sides started to tour the UK on a regular basis. As long as the Captain was blue-blooded and the Manager was English, it did not matter whether they knew the difference between a cricket bat and a tennis racquet. The composition of the team was largely dictated by the powerful Princely 'Dons' of cricket, and for the sake of respectability and communal harmony, one or two members of the minority communities were included.

Indian Princes continued to lead Indian teams until 1952, when Vijay Hazare led the side to England. On the '46 tour there is a lovely story about the great Merchant seeking Pataudi's advice on batting techniques on English wickets. Pataudi was obviously flattered until the day he mentioned this with pride to Amarnath, a man totally devoid of tact who never minces his words. He calmly informed his skipper that Merchant was making a fool of him since Merchant had already scored more than twice the number of runs that he, Pataudi, had on that tour!

In early 1934, at a mere suggestion from Anthony D'Mellow, who could well be called the father of Indian cricket, Bhupindersingh, the then Maharaja of Patiala, generously and spontaneously donated a gold trophy valued at £500 to be named after the great Ranji, who had passed away a year earlier. It is now established as the Ranji Trophy. It was to be competed for annually by the Provincial Associations of India.

The Jamsaheb of the erstwhile State of Nawangar entered his own team in the season of 1936–37, appropriately winning the trophy that year, for Nawangar was the principality over which Ranjitsinghji had ruled. Baroda was quick to follow, entering a team the following year, but getting knocked out in the very first match. Incidentally, this is the only erstwhile Princely State to have survived the ravages of time, and which still fields a side in the National Championships of India. Baroda has won the National Championship most times after mighty Bombay.

Wisden confirms that a world record partnership for any wicket in first-class cricket stands to its credit – 577 runs between Vijay Hazare and Gul Mahomed. Baroda has produced three Indian Captains, in addition to a long and distinguished list of players, both for India and Pakistan, and one family alone has supplied eight first-class cricketers, including an Indian Captain and an 'inefficient' Manager for an Indian team.

Other Princely States soon followed, prominent among these being Patiala and Indore (Holkar). The eighty-odd States in Western India were too small to enter separate teams but somehow managed to form themselves into a body with the name Western Indian States' Cricket Association. The Princely States found it difficult to raise teams of quality from within their own people and so they went shopping. The British Provinces could not match their buying power. Had it not been for the Princes many of these players would not have attained their national and international fame. The conditions attached to the job were simple and straightforward. Their duty was to play cricket, make their best efforts to win the Ranji Trophy, and to guide and coach promising local players. In return they received security, pensionable jobs, free accommodation and a status in life, generally a military rank or the post of ADC to the Maharaja.

Traditional Princely rivalries and jealousies had entered a new field. The sole objective was to win the championship at any cost, and if this was not possible at least the main rival had to be defeated. No holds were barred.

In the early years of the Championship when there were no regular umpires available it was left to the home side to provide two gentlemen wearing white coats. Nothing could have suited Princely designs better. Many who watched cricket during those early years just cannot understand, in fact are totally bewildered at the 'unseemly' agitation over the standard of umpiring today! Is the umpire at fault if a prominent player of the rival team is lacking in batting technique and keeps on letting the ball strike his legs? Is an umpire not justified in changing his decision after a batsman has been clean bowled or too obviously caught, especially if the batsman happens to be his Princely patron or a very prominent player? Who said that the poor quality of umpiring is because the monetary attraction was not high enough? In those early days the monetary attraction was so great that an umpire could easily afford to retire for life if all he did was to give one 'good' decision. For all that, runs did not easily flow from the Princely blade: it had to make contact with the ball. Thereafter it was not necessary for the ball to travel more than a few inches. The fielder would rush in to prevent a cheeky Princely single and in his enthusiasm would accidentally kick the ball over the boundary, sometimes even accidentally kicking it more than once. A Royal captain once refused to take his team out after tea break because an

opposing batsman was only nine short of Sir Donald Bradman's record of 452. On another occasion during one match when things appeared to be going against the home team, it was accidentally discovered by a member of the visiting side that in the height of summer it had rained overnight but very selectively, soaking only two spots, one at each end of the wicket. Unfortunately for the home team the visitor had gone to the ground early for a jog and discovered this strange phenomenon before the coir mat had been laid for the day's cricket.

While all this was happening I was a silent spectator. Unfortunately, by the time I was catapulted on to the Indian first-class cricket scene, many things had been straightened out, and yet until my dying day I shall carry the strong impression that I first played for the Baroda Cricket Association when I was barely sixteen simply because I happened to be the heir-apparent. Ironically, I put up some of my best performances that season, and the fact that there was no hankey-pankey left can be proved in that the future Ruler of Baroda, playing against Hyderabad in only his third or fourth first-class innings, was given out when he was just short of the coveted three figures. In the ultimate analysis one must surely come to the conclusion that the contribution made to the game of cricket by the Princes of India is unique, for surely India's proud position on the cricket map of the world owes a great deal to the Royal patronage extended by them. English cricket, too, has benefitted. A unique record which may never be surpassed is that only three Indians have played for England, all three were Princes, and all three have scored a century on their début – K.S. Ranjitsinghji, Prince Duleepsinghji and the late Nawab of Pataudi.

Looking back, it appears strange that, whilst the cricket scene on the Indian sub-continent was literally swamped by scions of Princely India, tragically Great Britain, the Head of the Commonwealth and spreader of a virus called 'cricket fever' has, even to the present day, been unable to produce a 'Royal' cricketer with even an apology for some cricketing ability!

A MOST HONOURABLE FOE

SIR ROBERT MARK

Was brought up in a strict cricketing atmosphere, the household barometer responding not to the weather but to the fortunes of Yorkshire. As a schoolboy in Manchester, to which city his father had emigrated, he rose to be vice-captain of cricket at William Hulme's GS, performing as 'a moderately unsuccessful medium-fast bowler'.

I was born in 1917 within walking distance of Old Trafford. My father, a Yorkshireman whose three great passions were Yorkshire cricket, Leeds United and his family, emigrated from Leeds to Manchester before the First World War. Four of his five children were Lancastrian by birth but two were girls, sort of extras, or sundries as the Aussies will have it.

Cricket reflected the pattern of our life in those days, as it does now. Gentlemen and Players. Only amateurs had their initials on the scorecards. For the professionals it was surnames only. They even entered the field through different gates. Odd to think that the lower end of the social scale included such immortals as Hobbs, Hutton, Rhodes, Hirst, Sutcliffe and that natural 'Gentleman', Hedley Verity. Not an initial among them! Not many of the Gentlemen of those days are remembered, and then, not always for achievement. No TV of course. The live audience was limited to the game itself. This did not prevent an immense following through Press and radio. The two most memorable scenes of rejoicing I can recall in almost forty years in Manchester were the sinking of the *Bismarck* and in 1953 the almost all-day partnership of Watson and Bailey which denied the Aussies what seemed a certain victory and ultimately led to our regaining the Ashes.

I was fifteen years old when the leg theory or bodyline tour threatened the dissolution of Empire. Sadly, perhaps, it did more than that. It strengthened a dubious precedent for the hostile, intimidatory bowling accepted as routine today.

Cricket in those days attracted the kind of loyalty given to a school, a regiment, a county, a country. Badly paid, poorly administered, with little or no PR skills, it nevertheless occupied a disproportionate place in the minds and enthusiasms of Englishmen of all ages. Television, money and a mixed society have changed all that. Skill has increased. The one day game has widened the repertoire of the most gifted players and attracted crowds and sponsors. But local associations and loyalties have weakened. Of the counties, only Yorkshire represents a community. And

they are surely a pitiful reflection of their great days. The remainder offer a galaxy of talent. Mercenaries, drawn from all over the world. We marvel at their ability, enjoy the entertainment they provide, but no longer associate them with the locality they represent.

I think it sad, too, that a Test match against the West Indies, a side of marvellous talents, if played at the Oval, Lord's or Birmingham, is nowadays enjoyed more at home on television, with the sound switched off.

Professionalism, having achieved much for the game and its

players, sometimes goes too far. The attempted intimidation of umpires and batsmen by verbal harassment, underarm bowling to deny an opponent a fair chance of victory, these show the less acceptable face of cricket, which, as a game, most people expect to demonstrate those things we most admire in sport – team spirit, fairness, good manners, and perhaps above everything else, having given our best, the ability to lose well and generously. I like to think that, for most players and spectators, those qualities are still paramount. Though happily played all over the world cricket was and is English. Not Scottish, Welsh or Irish, but English. Its influence on our way of life is tangible but impossible to define – though Neville Cardus and A. G. Macdonell both achieved deserved fame in trying. It's all summed up for me by an incident in June 1979.

I had gone to a cocktail party in Canberra hoping to meet one of the immortals, Jack Fingleton. I had seen him bat before the war and admired his books and commentaries. Like Richie Benaud, always competent, always fair. But I had never met him and so jumped at the opportunity. Alas, he wasn't there. He had suffered a heart attack and was in Woden Hospital. There I went the following day, presenting myself as just another of his many admirers. We talked for an hour and I came away with the happiest of recollections. Before I left Australia I received the following letter from his hospital bed. It's nice to think that peace and friendship between ancient and honourable foes does not have to be restricted to Christmas.

My dear Sir Robert.
  A line that I hope reaches you 'ere you fly off to say how much I have appreciated meeting you and to thank you most sincerely for your many kindnesses...
A game must be good to bring people together and maybe again it will rise from the ashes of Packer. I can well imagine your Dad and how you had to duck for cover when Yorkshire had a bad day. I have innumerable good friends in England and should you happen across them at any time do give them my fondest wishes. Especially Cyril Washbrook at Old Trafford... Please give my salaams to "999" and maybe in the future we will meet again. I sure hope so.
  Sincerely

  Jack Fingleton

I know of no better mix than Lancs and Yorkshire.

'PLAY AT 'EM'
JAMES PRIOR

A *keen schoolboy cricketer, he later played for Lords and Commons, and still does so provided he can field at long leg or third man and does not have to bend too much.*

I was taken over to Aldeburgh Lodge, near Aldeburgh, for my first term at prep school. The headmaster was very keen on cricket and that was one of the reasons why my father wished me to go there. He didn't care too much about my education but he certainly wanted me to have a good grounding in cricket.

On the first afternoon, when my parents were having tea with the headmaster, my father asked how much pocket money I should be given for the term. The headmaster thought for a moment and replied half-a-crown. My father duly handed it over. It was recorded in the 'bank' book. My parents departed and I was left to find my way round the school.

Shortly afterwards I saw the headmaster. 'Prior', he said, 'would you like to buy a cricket ball.' 'Yes, please, Sir', I replied. 'Well, I have one here. That will be half-a-crown.'

My pocket money for the whole term had disappeared on the first afternoon of the summer term. I don't think in fact that I kept the cricket ball long as I have no doubt it was pinched by some horrors further up the school – the ownership by small boys of cricket balls was generally a short-lived affair. Luckily for me, within three weeks I had developed measles and went home to recuperate for two weeks and of course at the same time to get some more pocket money.

But if that was an unfortunate first experience of buying cricket equipment, one can remember many very happy days of looking at bats in the Easter holidays, judging the amount of grain down the bat, the straighter the better to enhance the prospects of getting a good drive. And then spending hours and hours alternately oiling the bat and then banging a ball against it until by the time you arrived at school for the start of the summer term you were able to tell your friends that you had got a very good driver.

The most extraordinary bat I ever saw was Peter May's. I mean generally bats that you pick up in the club house or at school have lots of red marks all down their edges with a few in the middle. But Peter's bat was not at all like that. His just had a sort of dent in the middle where every ball had struck, and it was only when one saw his bat that one realized what a very great cricketer he was. His bat was always straight, reminding me again of my old schoolmaster who used to tell us boys to look at the sweaters of the old pros. The right elbows and the area round the right ribs would be worn into holes, caused by the constant friction between the elbow and the ribs as shots were always played keeping the right elbow tucked in.

My old headmaster, who rejoiced in the nickname of 'Spug', used to take boys in the nets for hours at a time. To start with he used to say: 'Now, boy, play forward', and regardless of where the ball pitched we used to play forward. Luckily many years of practice meant he had achieved a great degree of accuracy. After ten minutes or so of the forward stroke we changed to playing back and then onto the off-drive. More advanced boys were instructed in the 'mow' shot to leg, and on special occasions in the cut. The on-drive was not considered a suitable shot for boys.

My rather undistinguished cricket career was carried forward at Charterhouse by two people worthy of comment in any account of the game. R.L. Arrowsmith was in charge of the Under-16 side. His knowledge of cricket was encyclopaedic and only matched by his enthusiasm. He developed in one a respect for the game as it should be played, as a gentleman's game, and he gloried in its history and anecdotes. He used to teach Latin to a junior form, and as he arrived at the door of his classroom he took off his cap and aimed to throw it onto his chair. Life was more comfortable for us if there was an accurate landing.

The other character was George Geary who had a very distinguished career in Jardine's England side and also with Leicestershire. His advice in the nets was to move one's feet and 'play at 'em'. I don't think it did my cricket much good, but I've remembered it all my life and hopefully have been 'playing at 'em' ever since.

OLE BLUE EYES
LESLIE THOMAS

Confesses that his cricket career has hardly been first-class: 'When I could play the game – in my twenties – nobody wanted me to play. Now I am in my fifties I play for the Lord's Taverners in front of thousands.' These days, however, he enjoys his cricket more because he is not so serious about it. 'Once I would lose a week's sleep because I got a duck on a Sunday – with the result that I got another duck on the following Sunday.' Rates his best score as 53 versus Ian Botham's Somerset XI at Bath in 1984. In the same match he caught Botham off a skier but it went largely unnoticed because 'everyone had walked off to lunch.'

I knew him, of course, many years before he knew me. One summer just after the war I went to Lord's and climbed to what they used to call the 'free seats' under the Father Time clock. Len Hutton was batting at the Pavilion end. I forget the match now, but one over is painted on my memory. To each of the first five balls Hutton played an almost identical stroke, a drive which went either to mid-off or to cover point. It appeared that he rolled the ball out to them, first one fielder then the other, like a ritual. Neither had to move a fraction; he was just measuring up. The last ball of the over was sent with the same quietness, exactly bi-secting the distance between the two men. It struck the boards at the cover boundary with an echoing crack.

It's a long time ago now for both of us. The teenage watcher is middle-aged; the great batsman is long retired to his house and to his memories.

I missed no chance of seeing him at the wicket. In 1951 he made his hundredth hundred against Surrey at the Oval and on the Saturday evening he was not out. Early on the Monday I was in the queue as the sun came up over Kennington. A great crowd was assembled on the bank in front of Archbishop Tenison's school. Boys were standing on the school roof to watch. I had no fear of him failing. The bowler delivered the fateful ball and Len struck it with all his grand and lovely power to the fence.

In 1948 he scored 30 out of an England total of 52 in the Fifth Test against Australia. He stood, as though he did not quite understand, as batsman after batsman, Compton, Edrich and all, trudged to the Pavilion. It was the first Test match I had ever watched. For years I had waited to see Don Bradman and I only saw him face two balls. Eric Hollies bowled him with the second and I remember thinking: 'Hutton wouldn't have let me down like that.'

Years later I walked into the editor's office at the London *Evening News*, disgruntled and intent on giving my notice. Reginald Willis, a wonderfully wily man who knew the craft of turning away wrath, picked up a cricket bat from behind his desk and said: 'Look at this, Len Hutton made 364 with this in 1938.' He regarded me fiercely: 'Wouldn't like to work with him, would you?'

Of course I did. He had retired from cricket after becoming the first professional to captain England and was engaged to write his comments on the forthcoming series against Pakistan. I was to be his amanuensis. There is a story, and I've never asked Sir Leonard about it, concerning the day he was signed up to give his name to the column (it said: 'Sir Leonard Hutton was talking to Leslie Thomas' in small italics at the bottom). Having put his signature on the contract the great cricketer was led outside the building to be introduced to the motor car that was also part of the reward. I was not present at this ceremony but the tale went that having been shown the plush interior and the shining exterior by a whole pride of directors he smiled his small smile and said: 'Aye, very nice. Where's the wash-leathers?'

Some took this as evidence of extreme Yorkshire thrift and others as part of his methodical attention to the smallest detail which was always a factor in his life on the cricket field. (He once pointed out to the umpires that the pitch was several inches short and they had to prepare another.) Personally I can just see him making the remark about the wash-leathers and I am sure it was one of those moments of mischief in which he secretly delighted and which so many sober and earnest people took for gospel. I never knew him short of an answer. Years after he retired I was enjoying his company at a cocktail party given on the eve of an important one-day international to be played at Lord's. An eager young journalist, pad at the ready (padded up, you might say) asked: 'Sir Leonard, would you have liked to have batted in limited-overs cricket?'

'Oh, yes', came the careful reply. 'You always have a good excuse for getting out.'

As I got to know him I became familiar with the signs and when I have met him each summer, usually at Lord's, it has been a matter of delight to me that they are still in evidence. Hutton's creased face crinkles up a little, the on-going effect of the half-smile that issues from the edges of his mouth. He has the most amazing eyes of any man I have ever met, the most rivetting blue with flecks of deep humour in them. I have never been confronted with Sinatra but 'Ole blue eyes' can have little on Len of Pudsey.

On the first day I met him, when 'Sir Leonard Hutton Comments...' was to be published in the lunchtime edition of the *Evening News*, he did not turn up until the middle of the afternoon. Faced with this important absence I wrote a column on how wonderful it was to see Tom Graveney batting again. (The match was Worcestershire versus the Pakistanis and was Graveney's first game after he left Gloucestershire.) Some time after the lunch interval this long-overcoated figure materialized at the extreme end of the press box. He appeared in no hurry. His back had been bad, he explained. Nervously I showed him my 'Sir Leonard Hutton Comments' piece – a thousand words of thoughts and experiences from a man I had never met. 'Ah, yes', he nodded sagely. Those blue eyes turned up, smiling. 'That's just what I would have... er... commented'.

I liked him from that moment and I have never ceased to do so. Once his recurring back pain was so intense that, with help from two England cricketers, I had to carry him to his car. Sometimes I ended up driving it and I remember one occasion when he suggested that we should stop because he had spotted an old lady who wanted to cross the road. Naturally I was the one who got out to perform this chivalry. It turned out that she did *not* want to cross at all. Returning to the car, a little miffed, I told Sir Leonard what had happened.

'Dithering', he said. 'That's what caused run-outs in Test matches, you know. Dithering'.

During our summer working together I had my first play produced on television. Anxious that it should get as large a recommendation as possible, at least in my own paper, I spent one cricket lunchtime in the press box typing an essay in promise of its excellence. Sir Leonard watched me intently, biting away at a packet of sandwiches as he did so. Eventually, running out of superlatives, I went to the refreshment tent and bought two cups of tea and a packet of crisps. 'Those crisps look all right', he mentioned.

'Help yourself,' I said busily.

He did. 'They're better with salt', he suggested.

'Isn't there any salt?' I asked, still typing.

'Ah, right, there it is', he murmured. I was vaguely conscious of his disinterring the blue packet and spreading its contents on the crisps. He sampled the results and pronounced them excellent. While I typed he munched. Eventually when I looked at the packet there were only half a dozen miserable crisps left in the bottom. By this time I knew him well

enough to permit sarcasm. 'You might as well finish them off,' I said moodily.

'Oh no, lad,' he said, kindly patting my arm. 'You eat them. They're your crisps.'

He did it for the inward fun of it. I never heard him shout or laugh loudly. The joy was almost secret, shared only if you got to know him. Even now, when someone tells me a Hutton story, I can see the joke protruding, even if frequently they cannot. At Edgbaston, during one of the Test matches we covered together, a young reporter – once again figuratively padded up – approached with diffidence and, nodding at the play, asked: 'Sir Leonard, what do you think they're trying to do?'

With the world's most serious and obliging expression (the lad was from a *rival* newspaper, by the way) Hutton studied the middle for some time and eventually turned. The reporter's pen hovered.

'I think,' said the great man, 'they're trying to get them out.'

And the chap *wrote it down.* The expression of concern and truthfulness that occupied Hutton's face could convince anybody. Once at Trent Bridge I saw him demonstrating to an audience, which included Fred Titmus, John Murray and Barry Knight, how, in 1946, Ernie Toshack of Australia had consistently bowled at his legs. 'I moved over,' said Hutton, demonstrating with a shuffle how he shifted to his left. 'But he was still bowling at my legs. So I moved again, and then again.'

We stood, me and three England cricketers, taking in every word, while, according to the yarn Hutton was standing almost by the square-leg umpire and Toshack was *still* bowling at his legs – with the stumps standing unattended some yards away.

Sometimes when his back was not too bad, he used to bowl to me, in hotel corridors and such-like, with a paper ball tied with string and me with a newspaper as a bat. 'If you could only bat,' he would sigh, 'you'd have made a great tourist.'

His point was that, apart from cricketing ability, you had to be optimistic and resilient to tour abroad, particularly in Australia. He greatly admired Godfrey Evans. 'He'd be keeping wicket all day in Sydney, ninety-five in the shade, and never miss a thing,' he recalled. 'Like the rest he would stagger off the field, have a bath, get dressed, have a drink, sit down at the piano in the hotel and start to play. He was ready for the evening. That's what you need on tour.'

Up at Scarborough last season I told Godfrey Evans this story and he repaid me with one of his own. 'In the 1946 tour,' he said, 'Australia at Brisbane were several hundreds for one wicket. They went on and on piling up the runs and no-one looked like taking a wicket. It was as hot as hell too. At the end of one over Len said to me: 'Godfrey, I think we'll have to get them in run-outs.'

Sir Leonard was one of the adjudicators at that Scarborough

match but he was taken ill and had to go home. When I last saw him at Lord's, however, his eye, like that of Moses, was not dimmed. Irving Rosenwater, the cricket statistician, was telling him that his younger son, Sir Leonard's that is, had played in one match recognized as first-class. The figures man revealed it was East Africa versus MCC, at Nairobi on such and such dates, in such and such year, and proceeded to recite from memory the younger Hutton's batting and bowling figures in both innings. Rosenwater stepped back looking rather pleased at his feat.

Sir Leonard's eyes had small lights shining in them. He looked at me and I knew the signs. 'Well, well', he said kindly. 'You never know what your kids get up to, do you.'

All those years ago when the illustrious batsman and his journeyman scribe were travelling the cricket grounds of England, people would come up to Sir Leonard Hutton, seek to shake his hand and so often say: 'Len – you be given me such a great deal of pleasure.'

And that, too, goes for me.

STOLEN HOURS
WILLIAM DEEDES

Born in 1913, his first sight of first-class cricket was of Warwick Armstrong's Australians playing Surrey at The Oval in 1921. He is the great-great-great grandson of one of the five men who founded Kent's Band of Brothers. At the age of eleven, he secured Jack Hobbs's autograph.

It has been my experience, deplorably but I suspect not uniquely, that cricket tastes sweetest during stolen hours. I am not thinking about a day off from the office for 'grandmother's funeral' in order to go to Lord's. It is more subtle than that. Much of the cricket I have watched and still remember from years long past came at times when, glancing at my watch or prodded by a companion, I got a message from my conscience that I ought to be elsewhere. That is the moment when, perversely, the match comes alive, wickets fall or fieldsmen race.

The thought first came to me in the 1950s when I had an informal arrangement with a companion in the House of Commons. When during June or July the House had an all-night sitting (as it did quite often in those years), we would consult in the early morning at Westminster about what was on at Lord's.

We would get out of the Commons around 10 am warned by the whips to be back punctually at 3.45 pm – since the Government's tiresome business had not been disposed of – and head for St John's Wood. My companion was Christopher Hollis, then Member for Devizes and a passionate supporter of Somerset. I supported Kent. We tried to avoid matches which involved either county and so might strike a jarring note.

Usually we retired first to our respective homes for a bath and shave; but occasionally we had to give that a miss. They were not fussy about such things at the Lord's turnstiles. Then we would settle down in a stand and let the sunshine take hold of us – it seemed always a sunny day. Around noon we would consult. Would a glass of beer make us any snoozier than we already felt. We always agreed that it could not.

But the magic started to work in mid-afternoon when we looked

84

at our watches. 'Whips want us back!' Whatever the state of the
game, the cricket then became compulsive watching. That
was the pleasurable hour.

I think I was first corrupted by the stolen hours
doctrine while I was still at my preparatory school. My
father, not a keen watcher but a dutiful parent, took us to the
Oval to watch Surrey in some international match. I was
thrilled and before going to bed wrote my reflections on the
day, which I showed to my father. By a coincidence, he
had invited one of the younger masters at my school to
lunch a day earlier at the Hans Crescent Hotel, where
we were staying.

Asked what he would like to drink, this
innocent fellow chose a whisky and soda. 'And all of
two fingers,' (a recognized measure in those days) my
father afterwards exclaimed indignantly to my mother.
'I don't think much of a place where masters drink
like that.'

So when, tentatively, I proposed a second day at the Oval, though it meant a late return to school, my father replied injudiciously: 'No hurry to go back to that sort of place.' There was a row when I did get back, but that second day at the Oval produced wonderful cricket.

During much of my childhood A. P. F. Chapman, Cambridge, Kent and England, whose sad story was recently chronicled by a biographer, played for my home town of Hythe. Indeed his agreement to turn out for the side, particularly in Hythe Cricket Week, was part of the not very happy compact he made with Mr G. L. Mackeson, who owned the local brewery, was dotty on cricket, and gave him a job.

Percy Chapman, particularly when he was striking against modest club bowlers, was not a man you could leave unwatched. It was simply not possible while he was on the field to fulfil undertakings to be back home at appointed hours. In those days parents had absurdly old-fashioned ideas about punctuality at meals. It was never easy to describe, when you got back in time for the coffee, how many balls Chapman had hit out of the ground.

Stolen hours mix with cricket in many guises. To me the funniest passages in A. G. Macdonell's classic story about the village cricket match in *England, Their England* is not the blacksmith's bowling but the hours frittered away in pubs before the match begins.

I can testify from experience. When some of us joined the editorial staff of the *Morning Post* in the early 1930s, a condition of employment was willingness and ability to play in the newspaper's annual match against the editor's village of Dunmow in Essex. H.A. Gwynne, CH (no less) was strict about this. So strict that before the match some of us would go to the nets then run by an Australian, Alan Fairfax, in the basement of Thames House.

We then undermined this valuable practice on the journey to Dunmow. For in those days the road to Dunmow from London went through Benskins country, and they brewed incomparable beer. 'You fellows must be thirsty after your long drive,' Gwynne would say when we arrived suspiciously late for lunch and careful not to try to enunciate a word like 'suspicious'. 'Have a glass of sherry!' That and a glass of port after the lunch wiped out most of the benefits of Fairfax. Mercifully, our side included R.C. ('Crusoe') Robertson-Glasgow, the Somerset bowler, then the newspaper's cricket correspondent. For health reasons, he was supposed not to drink, and he bowled well enough to keep the rest of us our places on the staff.

Then there was a Monday in 1938, when I was persuaded not much against my will to go to Canterbury to watch Kent play against the Australians. This was Frank Woolley's last summer and his final appearance against Australia.

The Australians had spent Saturday scoring their runs. On

Monday Kent batted and before we had time to buy a scorecard and settle down, Woolley was out – for virtually nothing. I was due back in London after lunch, but as the Kent wickets fell it occurred to me that a follow-on was possible. I hung on guiltily in that expectation, which was fulfilled.

In the late afternoon light Kent batted again. I forget exactly how many Woolley scored: something like 70 out of 75. Much of the old grace and magic was restored to him for that short hour, When he was out, I see very clearly still the salute the Australians gave him as he left their playing fields for ever.

A year later, 1939, we had the West Indians with us. When they got to the Oval (Aug 19, 21, 22) time was running short for all of us. I felt drawn to this match. The difficulty was that on the day I chose to go galley proofs were awaiting my urgent attention in my newspaper office. Why urgent? Because the booklet I had written for them was about air-raid precautions.

From rather a good seat at the Oval I consulted my companion, Miss Rose Talbot, later of Malahide Castle and now resident in Tasmania. She was a matchless cricket-watching companion because she would speak only between overs, and then sparingly. She advised that the proofs ought to wait until stumps were drawn. So I stayed on to see amazing displays by Stollmeyer, Weekes and Constantine. That stolen hour had to last some of us for five years. In bad moments of the war I drew heavily on my memory of it.

THE AGE OF DENIS
DONALD STEEL

Used to be better at cricket than golf until he became professionally involved with the latter; played for Bucks and was selected once for Cambridge (but did not play). After that, was content to be an enthusiastic Crusader, making occasional Sunday appearances for Gerrards Cross. Now firmly on the retired list, but keeps in personal touch through cricket dinners.

Practically my only complaint about life in golf is that, for the last twenty-five years or so, contact with cricket has relied heavily on Johnners, Blowers and McGillers. Now, there is nothing wrong with that except that an absence from the direct scene of operations for so long hardly makes one ideally qualified to comment on contemporary matters in the game.

It would be nice to be able to claim televised highlights as a significant link but the BBC insists on showing them in the middle of the night; and, anyway, highlights have a habit of making the dullest day's play exciting. Yet that is perhaps the most accurate commentary on the change the game has undergone during that period. It has become more frenzied.

To some extent, this has been part of a prescribed plot. It has fallen under the spell of one-day cricket, Packer, commercialism, floodlit frolics and pitch invasions, but the price that has been paid has been a high one. It has surrendered so much of its dignity and its identity.

Happily the 1985 series with Australia marked some return to the days when the first ball of a Test match, that great moment, was watched in a deathly hush. There was little of the chanting and senseless can-rattling of recent years, slightly less even of the adulation amongst players for the simplest of catches which is as ridiculous as seeing batsmen booted, spurred, padded and helmeted against the feeblest of attacks.

On a rare visit to Fenner's a few years ago, I wondered what

Douglas Jardine would have thought of a county opening pair venturing forth like astronauts on a pitch on which no University bowler was ever likely to get the ball above waist high. Helmets have made cricketers as hard to distinguish as American footballers; and, for what? The worst accident for years was made worse by a helmet. They can make players more inhibited rather than less.

You could always tell Len Hutton by the way he twiddled his cap or cradled his bat. Keith Miller was instantly recognizable for the imperious brush of his uncontrollable mane. Peter May, on the other hand, never had a hair out of place, and the faster and shorter you bowled to Bill Edrich, the harder he hooked.

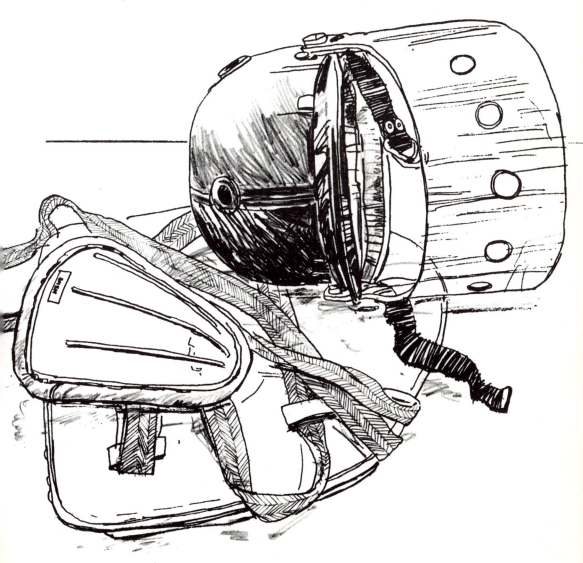

They would have regarded recourse to a helmet as a sign of weakness. Viv Richards has no truck with one and Ian Botham always seems to me to bat better and more definitely when bare-headed. There was one occasion at Old Trafford in 1948 when Denis Compton mishooked a bouncer into his forehead and another when Miller caused him to topple onto his stumps in sepulchral light at Trent Bridge. But he came back to make 145 not out at Manchester, scored 184 at Nottingham and even when out of form managed to make failure seem acceptable – at least to his legions of admirers of whom I was the greatest.

The reassuring thing is that, over the last thirty years, no other cricketer has shared enough of the same heroic mould for me to contemplate a transfer of allegiance. To be the perfect hero, a player must combine unusual playing talents with a fun-loving, chivalrous approach. Never, by word or deed, did Compton betray such ideals. Not for him an angry word or bad-tempered gesture. Even his barren times never cast a shadow for long.

In that incomparable joking way of his, John Warr suggested that when Compton occupied the chair in *Mastermind*, he should take as his specialist subject 'My great Test innings on the Australian tour of 1950–51'. Whereas, in the State games, he could do no wrong, his highest score in eight Test innings was 23. Warr, Compton's biographer in the *World of Cricket*, struck the right degree of seriousness when he wrote: 'He had a strangely plebeian start when he should, in the light of future events, have been borne down from Valhalla on a silver cloud.' However, to my mind, London Transport acted with great foresight by having the No 13 bus terminated at Hendon and routed past Lord's; so it was by this means that he arrived there to make a hundred on his first appearance for the Elementary Schools Under 15 side against Mr C.F. Tufnell's XI, opening the innings with Arthur McIntyre, later to become an equal stalwart for Surrey.

There was only one course after that. Denis served his apprenticeship on the ground staff, gained his place in the full Middlesex side and graduated to play for England at the age of 19, becoming the youngest Englishman to make a century against Australia. It is almost unthinkable nowadays for a nineteen-year-old to play for England but Compton is not one to whom general rules apply.

He once made 300 in South Africa in one minute over three hours – the same time that is considered fairly normal to make 50 in India. In 1948, he and Bill Edrich set a new third-wicket record for Middlesex by making 424 against Somerset, the last 209 coming in 70 minutes, 139 of them to Compton. The previous summer, when Middlesex won the Championship, Edrich and Compton opened the second innings at Leicester, scoring the 66 needed to win in 25 minutes with four minutes to spare. In the first innings, they had made 257 and 151 and throughout the summer set records that will never be broken.

When both had their eye in, nobody could set a field to them and a mischievous picture is conjured up of opposing bowlers doing everything they could to escape the nod from their captain. However, Compton (and Edrich, for that matter) never lacked the courage or technique to play defensive innings and many of Compton's finest innings were on pitches of doubtful character.

It is interesting, though hardly surprising that Peter May should pay him the compliment of writing in his recent autobiography, *A Game Enjoyed*: 'I still marvel at his method, a model to any young batsman because he played so straight – and not only in defence. His genius is that he had so many improvisations on a basic soundness.'

It is even true to say that he played his famous sweep with an almost straight bat but how glad he must have been of his powers to improvise when he became stricken by damaged knees. Nobody else could have overcome such a handicap; yet he was always, it seems, making his return after operations with innings for every occasion. Finally in 1956, recalled by England, he hit 94 and 35 not out against the Australians at the Oval. After he was fourth out in the first innings, the remainder added only 25. Knee-caps or none, it was an astonishing performance.

Earlier in the sober post-war days, there was only one hero for enthusiastic young cricketers. Compton provided the extravagance that could have filled Lord's twice over, weaving his magic in a manner that revived the meaning of happiness. As a schoolboy, there was always the feeling that you might miss something and, however much time there may have been to spare, the walk from St John's Wood station could never be completed quickly enough. If you did arrive late, the first thing was to look if No 4 was on the scoreboard.

The Lord's switchboard was often jammed by people asking the same question and the taxi-drivers did a roaring trade rushing those from the City who suddenly found they had important business in NW8. There were no rations in an innings by Compton. Each stroke bore the mark of genius – instinctive and free. He was too much of an artist to become enslaved by a bowler, too much of an independent spirit to allow bowlers to dictate the terms. He called the tune and, though his career ended before the advent of limited-over cricket, his talents may have been even more suited to a style that cries out for the unconventional. A cross-batted slog would never have done for him.

No cricketer has been so much loved as Denis in his heyday – certainly not since. People worshipped him because they saw in him the batsman they would so like to have been. In a golfing context, he was Severiano Ballesteros or Arnold Palmer. He had the gift of identifying himself with those watching. You played his innings with him and, if there was the odd hiccough between the wickets, this merely added to the fun, but Compton's accomplishments were not confined to the crease.

In his younger days, before his knees started to plague him, he was a dashing outfielder and later, when pensioned off at slip, he could interrupt learned discussions with Edrich or Godfrey Evans to catch most of what came his way.

If he had never made a run, he could have held his own for Middlesex as a left-arm spinner. Altogether, he took 617 wickets and should have won a Test match, an historic Test match, as a bowler. Although not a man given to regrets, it must still be a bitter disappointment that he did not. On the final day at Leeds in 1948, when Australia made 404 for 3 for victory, the pitch was tailor-made for spin, the leg and googly spin, or left-arm equivalent, which Denis delivered off no more than two or three paces. He sent down his overs in double-quick time; so fast, in fact that you wondered if even he knew what was coming next. When you think how much play is wasted nowadays watching fast bowlers walk back to begin endless run-ups, the memory is refreshing. It was nothing in those days to get through 90 overs before tea; but I digress.

Compton could really tweak the ball from the back of the hand and at Leeds he got plenty of response. He caught and bowled Lindsay Hassett, lured Arthur Morris yards out of his ground only to find that, for once, Godfrey Evans was all thumbs, and then had to endure the sight of Jack Crapp twice put down gentle dollies at slip off the bat of a bamboozled Don Bradman. If Bradman and Morris had followed Hassett, England would surely have been home. As it was, the Australians, sensing the threat, decided at lunchtime that Compton had to be hit out of the firing line. This he duly was and Norman Yardley, the England captain, was not enough of a gambler to lead trumps again.

One other factor which added to Compton's heroic image was that he was international class as a footballer, winning FA Cup and League Championship medals with Arsenal. Nowadays the overrunning of both seasons makes this impossible but the first of two innings which I remember most vividly, played ten years apart, took place within a few days of his reporting back for duty to Highbury.

In some ways, the first was a let-down. Needing one more century to equal Jack Hobbs's record of centuries in a season, he was bowled by Jack Ikin for 17. I had gone to see history made and I have never forgiven Lancashire for delaying the inevitable in a match watched, incidentally, by 60,000 over the three days. However, next day (when I couldn't be present), he made amends with 139 and ten years later, on August 28 1957, he made 143 on his farewell for Middlesex against Worcestershire.

Three days earlier, in a memorial match at Ashtead, he batted against a modest club attack and fielding side which had to work honourably hard to allow him to reach 40. That was typical of Compton; as, indeed, was his parting gesture at Lord's.

After his century in the first innings, 48 may not seem much but it showed that neither age nor injury could daunt his skill. He departed to a catch in front of the committee room (where else?) by Laddie Outschoorn, his distinctive walk taking him back to the custody of the pavilion for the last time, bat held aloft. As he climbed the steps and disappeared from view, there was already a sense of loss but at least he was allowed to return in peace and lone glory. Those modern spectators who rush on to the field and force players to run for dear life deprive the game of its special moments – none more special than this.

ONE, TWO, THREE....
OUT!
BRIAN REDHEAD

Universally known to be Geoffrey Boycott's number one fan. Thinks highly too of Sunil Gavaskar and Phil Edmonds, from which it will be deduced that he most admires those cricketers who are their own men. Has retained a special affection for Lancashire CCC and Clive Lloyd, who for many years was a near neighbour.

I was the best spin bowler in our street, when I was eight.
It was not difficult to be the best spin bowler in our street because there were only four of us who played cricket and I was the only one who bowled spin. Billy preferred to bowl fast, Kenny preferred to bat, and Trevor kept wicket and kept score. Trevor is now a Director of Education.

To bowl spin at all, however, was an achievement because we played with a rubber ball in the street, not on the pavement where the lines between the flag-stones might have re-directed the bounce, but in the middle of the road on the asphalt. My father had drilled three holes in a hard wood block and we placed that in the centre of the carriageway with the stumps inserted and the bails on. Motor vehicles seeking access had to wait until the end of the over. Most of the visiting vehicles were used to our ways and would wait patiently but an occasional stranger would hoot and rage and be rewarded by the cold hard stares of four implacable eight year-olds. My mother always said that if Hitler himself had come up the street in his armoured car he would have been quelled by us. We took our cricket very seriously.

With much licking of the fingers, twitching of the wrist, and limitless optimism, I persuaded both myself and more importantly the batsman that I could bowl both off-breaks and leg-breaks, and I was top of the Bruce Gardens bowling averages every season, as Trevor affirmed. In one famous Test match – Trevor and me versus Billy and Kenny – I clean-

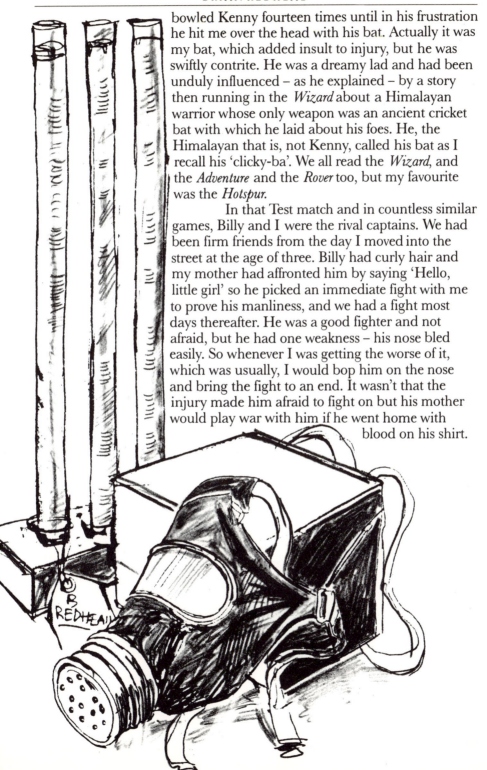

bowled Kenny fourteen times until in his frustration he hit me over the head with his bat. Actually it was my bat, which added insult to injury, but he was swiftly contrite. He was a dreamy lad and had been unduly influenced – as he explained – by a story then running in the *Wizard* about a Himalayan warrior whose only weapon was an ancient cricket bat with which he laid about his foes. He, the Himalayan that is, not Kenny, called his bat as I recall his 'clicky-ba'. We all read the *Wizard*, and the *Adventure* and the *Rover* too, but my favourite was the *Hotspur*.

In that Test match and in countless similar games, Billy and I were the rival captains. We had been firm friends from the day I moved into the street at the age of three. Billy had curly hair and my mother had affronted him by saying 'Hello, little girl' so he picked an immediate fight with me to prove his manliness, and we had a fight most days thereafter. He was a good fighter and not afraid, but he had one weakness – his nose bled easily. So whenever I was getting the worse of it, which was usually, I would bop him on the nose and bring the fight to an end. It wasn't that the injury made him afraid to fight on but his mother would play war with him if he went home with blood on his shirt.

Billy and I were inseparable. We went to nursery school together, in the Congregational Church hall at the top of Two Ball Lonnen. One day there we built a wigwam out of the chairs and invited a fat boy whom we disliked to enter it. When he went in Billy pulled the bottom chair away and the whole thing fell upon the hapless child. Billy is now a Director of Municipal Housing in Canada.

One day at infants' school the teacher invited the boys in the class to make wooden swords saying that she would choose the best for the play. Billy and I rushed home at dinner time. I bolted my meal and then set to work in the garage. I called on Billy as usual to go back to school but he had already gone and I guessed why. I raced to school to find him waiting at the gate with a smirk from ear to ear. 'I've given teacher my sword,' he said, 'and she likes it.' I rammed mine right up his nose and he bled all over his Aertex.

Two days before the outbreak of the Second World War we were evacuated – Billy and me, and Trevor and Kenny, and several million other children. We had our clothes in our satchels, our gasmasks round our necks, and a label each in case we got lost. They also gave us a carrier bag each containing our iron rations. We four went with the school and our teacher Mr Graham on a train from Scotswood in Newcastle to Dalston on the coast of Cumberland. There we were dispatched in bus loads, one bus to each village. They lined us up in the village school room and took their pick. Billy and I were the last to be chosen. With obvious reluctance the local sub-postmaster agreed to take us and promptly displayed our iron rations on a shelf in his shop and sold them. He would have sold us too given the chance for he didn't like us and we didn't like him. After an unruly month we were rescued and sent to live in separate farm houses, but we still spent most of our waking lives together, playing and fighting.

In the summer of 1940, with the scholarship safely behind us and our academic futures determined, we played cricket at school day in and day out. The final match of that golden summer was more important to us than a Test match. This was no limited-over picnic, this was a fight to the death, even if it meant being late for tea. Billy and I captained the opposing teams and on paper his was the better side. I won the toss and chose to bat arguing that the wicket would take spin in the second hour. We were all out for 27, more than enough I assured my team. When they were 19 for 7 – Redhead at that point having taken 6 for 4 – I was still confident. But Billy was still in, the only man in either team to have reached double figures. He was blocking my every ball, and making hay at the other end against a bowler who could only bowl underarm. Two he scored and then a four off the last ball of the underarm's over. 25 for 7. I was desperate. In fact as I walked back to my mark I was close to tears and wondering if I could take three wickets before Billy got at the other bowler again. I ran up for the first ball of the over and just as I brought my arm over I noticed that Billy in his enthusiasm had moved out of his crease. I brought my arm full circle and whipped off his bails.

'Howzat,' I roared confidently.

The umpire, Mr Graham, was non-plussed. He was not all that familiar with the laws of cricket.

'Rule a hundred and twenty-three, Sir,' I shouted – 1, 2 and 3 being the numbers I first thought of.

Mr Graham hesitated.

'The ball is deemed to be in play,' I invented hastily, 'when the bowler's arm comes over even if it has not left his hand, Sir.'

Mr Graham looked at me and knowing I now suspect how much it meant to me not to lose that game raised his index finger. Billy opened his mouth to protest, thought better of it – you didn't argue with the teacher in those days – and stomped off. I clean-bowled the next two and that was it.

Six weeks later Billy and I went our separate ways to different secondary schools. I played lots more school cricket, but it never mattered as much again to win, and I never again invoked Rule 123.

CRICKET IN CORFU
LORD ORR-EWING

At Trinity College, Oxford, played (twice) for the Authentics, and for the Trinity Triflers (a side which toured surrounding villages). Later, until the outbreak of war, he played country-house cricket. On becoming an MP in 1950, he was persuaded to take up the game again, and has played every year since then for the Lords and Commons, keeping wicket for 15 seasons. Since 1965 has organized matches against the clubs in Corfu, and has been President of the Anglo-Corfiot Cricket Association since it started in 1970.

This summer in Corfu we have been celebrating the 150th anniversary of the first Corfiot v Corfiot cricket match. The history of cricket in Corfu, since its initiation in 1814 when the island came under British protection, has been well covered in the coloured booklet *Corfu and Cricket* published by the Anglo-Corfiot Cricket Association (ACCA). It is my task to cover the more recent progress and, more particularly, the September Festival of 1985.

In 1983 the Esplanade ground in Corfu was grassed over for the second time in a decade. The routine after-care, rolling and mowing, seems to have been spasmodic, since the grass is sparse and in no way compares with the lovely sward achieved on the golf course. The matting wicket has been replaced with a soft concrete. The new wicket gives more normal, though lower, bounce, and front-foot players greatly enjoy themselves. It is safer than the matting on top of the hard concrete, on which the ball often reared steeply. I didn't witness the degree of spin which this wicket takes, since, during the six matches I watched, not one spinner on either side got an over. Each ball made a small indentation, so that a new surface may be needed next season.

The standard of Corfiot cricket has steadily risen, and their fielding, catching, throwing and enthusiasm are a great encouragement. Any profits from the sale of our booklet will help coach young Corfu cricketers. Past coaching has set an example, and improved their batting standards. Their umpiring has also greatly improved. A few years ago, if any ball hit any part of a batsman, 11 Corfiots and 90 per cent of the crowd shouted 'How-dat'. Intimidation by volume generally produced the desired result. I received an urgent message to take out five copies of Tom Smith's latest book *Umpiring and Scoring*, and I passed these over to Pipos Christou, an ex-policeman and cricketer, who is now their doyen of umpires. I think we can expect a continued improvement.

Although the cricket standard has improved, some of the infrastructure has sadly faded away. During the festival they used to erect a rented pavilion, which flew the Greek and British flags. This was not provided. The usual large display boards, advertising all the festival matches, were also absent. In the early days of the festival, cars and coaches were parked right up to the new fence which has been erected between the grass and the tarmac. The tarmac still forms part of the playing area, so that fieldsmen were crawling under cars whilst runs were still being taken. In latter days the parking improved, but the boundaries need to be clarified. I think the complete lack of publicity considerably affected the size of the crowds. With so many British visitors on the island they would have enjoyed the entertainment, had notices been posted in all their hotels.

There may be some who believe that the game of cricket is an imperial legacy which does not deserve encouragement. Since virtually every world sport, including soccer, rugger, tennis and golf, came from Imperial Britain, this is a weak argument, and certainly not held by SEGAS (the Greek Government's Sports Council), which does give local support and funds to Corfu cricket. ACCA has always believed that money spent on practice nets in a corner of the Esplanade would do more than anything else to spread local interest and encourage the next generation.

There are now four active local clubs (Byron, Gymnastikos, Phaex and Ergaticos) playing matches from early May until mid-October. Visiting teams normally play one match against each, and a final 'Test match' against their combined strength. Several teams which cannot stay a fortnight, play three matches in a week. In 1985, visiting teams included The Athens Ramblers, UCL Academicals, Hong Kong CC, The Cricket Society, a Dutch Flamingos XI, British Airways, and Elmstead CC. In addition, I organized and captained a scratch XI, which played against an All-Corfu XI in the middle of September.

All matches are limited to 33 overs for each side. They are due to start at 2.30. Shortly after this, the Corfu captain courteously inquired of me whether I preferred to bat or field. As many cricketers are not experienced in batting in a temperature of 100 degrees, or on a concrete wicket, the visitors often select to field first, check the form and imbibe the atmosphere, whilst their supporters do the same with the ouzo. My match didn't start until 3.10, and I didn't immediately appreciate that my later batsmen would be groping in the dusk unless we finished by 7.30. Three of my later batsmen were totally unable to see the ball, and as the overs ran out mid-wicket conferences made each over last six minutes or more. Fortunately, the light equally handicapped their wicket-keeper, and our last eight runs came in byes. John Forte and Ben Brocklehurst both claim that on one occasion lighted candles were put on top of each stump. Bill Edrich once appealed against being dazzled by car headlights.

The Cricket Society's fortnight ended as I arrived. Chris Box-Grainger (the Vice-President) and Jeremy Burford reported that seven matches had ended with three wins and three losses. The crowd for their final 'Test match' on a Sunday was considerable, and was well rewarded with many sixes and a home win by five runs. In their series, Tony Crocket and Warwick Jordan both got undefeated centuries. Takos Bogdanos is the local Botham and got 40 or 50 in several of the matches, each of these being scored in about twenty balls. Bladon Lines had presented a splendid trophy, to be played for each year in the final match between the Society and All-Corfu. This was duly handed over at a celebration dinner.

I arrived on a Monday, when in the twenty-four hours 95 other

Jumbo jets and 15,000 British visitors also arrived, and I had a week in which to collect a scratch side from this material. Fortunately, the Flamingos XI was playing a full series and I was able to study their form. I signed up their opening batsman Hans Floberg, and opening swing bowler Edward Kruseman. I found a further clutch of cricketers staying at a hotel which is owned by Arie Bogdanos at Pyrgi and is now very successfully run by the Bladon Lines organization. Tony Jones, an old friend of my electronic industry days, was also staying there, and he agreed to act as my shop steward. He gathered a valuable five and two reserves. A Corfu Villa establishment at Nissaki yielded three more young men. Whilst peddling our booklet round the ground, I found Mike Steel, who captained the Wigan CC. He opened my batting and took two valuable wickets. Our Flamingos bowler removed their first four batsmen whilst the ball still had shine, and we got them all out for 144 in 30 overs. Their captain, Spiros Kantaros, made an excellent 61. Hans Floberg opened, and had made 89 when we won by 3 wickets, with an over to spare. I was glad to win, since John Forte, who knows the cricket form to a T, had forecast a nasty defeat. After forty years and two hip operations, he has hung up his boots, but he and his wife Nadia gave valuable advice and support. Immediately we finished in the gloom, a host of young schoolchildren ran on to the square to practise bowling and batting. Their enthusiasm shows the potential keenness and talent available.

At 9.30 we reassembled, as guests, for a gigantic meal and lavish drinks in a local taverna, curiously named Uncle Tom's Cabin. The Flamingos, having won all four matches, had lost their final against All-Corfu and handed over their impressive silver trophy, and I presented four ACCA ties to the most deserving. In his speech the Sports Council representative, Anastasios Calogheros, emphasized how anxious Greece was to have their cricket recognized as worthy of and qualifying as an Associate Member of the International Cricket Conference. In replying, I said that I would do my best but there were still several matters to be put right.

During my second week, British Airways XI had a most successful short tour. They won their two club matches but lost against All-Corfu. Gordon Abbott, who has long been a loyal member of the ACCA Committee, was helping with the speeches and organization at a wonderful reception they gave at the Corfu Palace. British Airways have always been a source of great encouragement.

The Greeks have always been highly political people, but Corfu hitherto has been relatively immune. Now, even this island is feeling some of the impact. The 150th anniversary reminded me yet again that cricket has a special place on this island, and, given continued encouragement from Britain, I am sure their enthusiasm can be made to overcome any temporary problems.

A COUNTY PLAYER

JEFFREY ARCHER

Born in Somerset, he spent many hours as a child recording the disastrous feats of the county in his *Playfair* scorebook, and assumed he would be required one day to play for them. He was educated at Wellington School before going up to Brasenose College, Oxford, where he won an athletics Blue. Despite later successes in the House of Commons and as a novelist, he remained surprised that the Somerset selectors should have failed to contact him, until one day...

When I was seven years old, a proper age to start one's love of cricket, I watched my home county, Somerset, skittled for 36 against Surrey.

I still expected, with schoolboy fervour, that we would remove the county champions for 35 when we took to the field.

P.B.H. May thought nothing of my opinion and scored an untroubled century, which I reluctantly acknowledged in my Playfair scorebook.

Neville Cardus, writing in the *Manchester Guardian* the next morning said of my heroes: 'Somerset, they toil not neither do they spin.'

Five years later, with Somerset remaining at the foot of the County Championship table on every intervening year, I assumed it would only be a matter of time before I ended up playing for my county.

By the time I was 17, Somerset had climbed to third place in the Championship table, so I took up athletics.

When I had reached the age of 27 and had run for Britain for the last time, Somerset were third again, so I retired with only the fantasy of playing cricket for my county.

At a dinner in honour of Viv Richards in London last year, I remarked during my speech that I still awaited the selectors' call for

Somerset and England.

It raised ironic cheers and laughter, as it became clear that many in the audience shared my fantasy.

I returned home to find a letter from Roy Kerslake, the Somerset chairman, inviting me to play for my county in a testimonial match for Richards. I accepted by return of post, first-class stamp, recorded delivery.

The match I had been selected to play in was to be at Warborough, and for a month before I trained hard in the nets during the week and with my local village side at the weekend.

When the great day came I was every bit as nervous as if it had been the Olympic trials.

The ground was packed and Somerset, having lost the toss, were invited to bat first. I had studied the scorecard. I was No 6: Roebuck, Denning, Rose, Richards, Botham, Archer. No wonder the opposition were terrified.

I strolled around the ground signing autographs, ignoring the little boy who, studying my signature wedged between Richards and Botham, said in a voice that carried: 'Never heard of him.'

When Brian Rose was stumped, Richards went to join Botham at the crease. I returned to the pavilion, shaking like a leaf. I padded up praying for a thunderstorm. But the sky was uncommonly clear.

While selecting a willow, I heard a scream from the crowd, Botham had been caught on the deepest boundary.

I allowed him to leave the pitch before appearing, and then walked slowly out of the pavilion to join the greatest batsman in the world.

He smiled and said: 'Watch the ball carefully for a couple of overs.' I grinned back. I did not expect to last a couple of overs.

A. E. LEWIS

Ted Dexter
Colin Cowdrey

Viv Richards.
Jeffrey Archer
Ian Botham

VIV RICHARDS TESTIMONIAL
SOMERSET.
WARBOROUGH.

I took guard, the only thing I could do with any confidence and survived 17 balls, in which time the score had advanced by 29. Richards had scored 26 and I had scored three from a thick edge over the slips.

I prefer not to dwell on the fact that during my first over I nearly ran the great man out and was informed testily by a yokel that the last stoning in Warborough had been in 1623.

On the 18th ball, my stumps were shattered by a slow straight delivery. The crowd's applause as I made my way back to the pavilion was generous in the circumstances.

At tea, Somerset declared with 318. Joel Garner and Hallam Moseley were given the new ball and battled away for six overs, failing to take a wicket, so Vic Marks was selected as the first change bowler.

Marks also failed to make the necessary breakthrough, so naturally the skipper tossed the ball to me. I dropped it.

The opposition scored two off my first over and three off my second. The fourth ball of my third over was short on the off side and was slipped to the boundary for four.

The next ball pitched in the same place, and I covered my eyes as the opening batsman shaped to repeat the shot, but Peter Roebuck had already moved several yards to his right in anticipation and took a superb catch on his boots. I had removed the opening batsman.

I leapt in the air with delight and looked forward to my next over, only to discover that Colin Dredge was removing his sweater and polishing the ball.

Disappointed, I returned to the boundary and as I passed Brian Rose he remarked: 'One for nine. You can live with those figures for the rest of your life.'

He's right, but I still sit by the phone on a Sunday morning before every Test match, waiting for P.B.H. May to call...

THE YEAR BEFORE THE WAR

EDWIN BROCK

ike most English grammar schoolboys his education consisted of RRRCF (the three Rs, Cricket and Football). The school was Alleyn's, and just down the road at Dulwich College Trevor Bailey already had one foot on the glory ladder. One wet Wednesday afternoon his school played the College at <u>football</u>. Bailey was in their team, Brock played for Alleyn's and they lost by a cricket score. On that day Brock touched <u>his</u> peak of cricketing glory, and 'since then it's been all downhill'.

He carried the score in his head
from radio to radio, like milestones
through the three days. It was
August in the long school break
and the sun shone from Heber Road
to Dulwich Park as it had always done
on running games and trees that
were stepped enough to climb.

And just up the road, a little
further than his boundaries, but
known from the top of a swaying
Victoria tram, small white figures
ran on the grass and made history.

The fretwork fronts of the radios
were galleons, or the sun going down
on the Empire: Marconi and Ecko,
Bush and HMV, all tuned to the same
few voices; listening posts on the air
that was making England between eleven
and lunchtime, lunchtime and tea.

Later, the war blotted it out,
as though a cleaver had cut clean
across all that came after boyhood.
But then, when barrage balloons were
not even dreaming, Hobbs and Hammond,
Bradman and Larwood were the names
they claimed to make their games of
chalk wickets and old grey tennis balls.
Hutton had not entered that mythology:
he was the bit of history they bumped into.

Through quiet chinks in a long cacophony
the commentators brought them out. It was
a year of stiff-armed salutes and shrieking voices;
of a father beginning a journey that
did not end, and an iron gate clanging shut.

It was a Saturday at the end of the summer-
break, and the days were tearing away
like a grownup's temper. It was the
Timeless Test: 'What if it lasts a month!'
they said. 'What if it lasts till Christmas!'

He knew Edrich as he knew Hobbs and
Hammond, Larwood and Bradman, from
the backs of the cigarette cards they
read and then flicked in gambling games.
He heard them come out. He heard them begin.
And then he ran in the streets and forgot them.

At teatime he eased the sweat-wet shirt
from his back and remembered. Edrich had gone
but England were 374 for 1. He ate bread
and jam, drank tea, grabbed a ball and ran out.
'I bags I'm Len Hutton!' he shouted.

Sunday was a killjoy day of best clothes
and a thick ear if you tore them. The streets
were empty, so he walked to the dogpond at
Peckham Rye and watched long-haired mongrels
who belonged to no-one chase quietly collared
bitches of recognizable breeds. He jumped back
as they shook black-green water everywhere
and brushed splashes from his clothes.

He watched a strange boy leap from the pondside
to a drain six feet out. It was easy. They
did it in turns until his foot slipped and
he sat in the stagnant water. The strange boy
ran away and he walked slowly towards punishment.
The Test was tomorrow and school the day after.

On his last day of freedom he counted
the lamp-posts, the trees, the telegraph poles
and avoided all the cracks in the pavement.
By the time fifteen men had disturbed
the pigeons at the Oval, the bushes in
Dulwich Park were noisy with schoolboys.

That day names fell from their cigarette
cards onto the Oval grass: Hammond
and Hardstaff, Paynter and Compton.
And calling the names out made them feel famous.

They heard the score shouted by park-
keepers and from shops walking home.
It did not interfere with their playing
but they tucked it away, comfortable
at winning. And, as the day shone on,
even the grownups became excited.

Stumps were drawn as he ate his tea:
Hutton was 300 and Bradman's record 34 away.
He did not believe it would be broken:
Bradman was always, like Bluebird or Tommy Farr.

After nearly fifty years he remembers
only that it happened when he was there
and that he found it lost among old
dance songs and his short running breath.

Each stroke had sent the present searching
into the past where it was recovered and recorded.
Eleven Australians tried to stop it, there and then,
dead at one moment on a summer's afternoon.
But it went on until it was claimed and written
and talked about and became the year before the war.

A FIXTURE TO FORGET
BASIL BOOTHROYD

Claims to have no cricketing history beyond sitting next to Denis Compton's table in a famed Fleet Street wine bar. Offers, instead, his most valuable cricketing experience, which arose from telling a man at a party that he was to speak at a Kent CCC dinner. The man begged him to get Alan Knott's autograph for his young son. He did so, and sent the signature on. The man, after expressing eternal gratitude, later turned up locally as Boothroyd's bank manager.

I only once played for England. A proud moment, and that was just about how long it lasted. This devious Dutchman lobbed me a sitter. Lbw first ball. Spectators barely had time to take in my classic stance, borrowed boots, and the way I wore my collar pulled up at the back like Bradman.

If you're no cricketer, I always say, at least try to give the illusion. Goodness, I've seen men make a double century looking like nothing on earth, their trousers not even decently tucked under the bottom pad-strap. A disgrace to the game.

I didn't think of myself as playing for England. None of us did. Just for a side assembled by *Punch* magazine to meet the over-forties of The Hague and show them where they got off. It was their sports-writers who gave us the glorious label in the Saturday evening headlines. 'ENGLAND THRASHED', they said. In Dutch, naturally, but we weren't short of willing interpreters.

Recalling my one-day overseas tour I sometimes tell people that I went out of literary curiosity, curious to learn the Dutch for English cricketing terms. Indeed I did that, and it was disappointing. As an example, the Dutch for lbw is lbw. Or I tell them I wanted to investigate the comical rumour that cricket was in fact played at all in Holland.

Even before we saw them in action, this proved no rumour. When they met us in force off the boat they mustered a radiance of honorary club ties, from Free Foresters to I Zingari. And these were only the oldies, more or less dug out of retirement to give us a game. The Hague's serious business, it seemed, was conducted by about six elevens of the lusty and unwrinkled, who spent half their summers meeting the smarter clubs across the water, and probably thrashing them.

All we could raise between us, in the way of sartorial signals, was our captain's Staffordshire cap: which brings me to a correction. I said the *Punch* side had been assembled. Too casual, that sounds. It had actually been press-ganged. Our captain, Bernard Hollowood, was also our editor. Cricket had ruled his life. His, his brothers', and their father's before them. They all played for Staffordshire in their time, Bernard himself a mighty amasser of runs, who not only looked like a cricketer but was one. When the old man died, he once told me approvingly, one of the brothers following him to his last rest stopped to thumb the churchyard turf. 'They'll turn today', he said.

So you see the situation. Artists and writers regularly in the pages of *Punch*, and anxious to keep things that way, would have been crazy to decline selection for the Dutch treat, though most of us could have in honesty claimed that we hadn't held a bat for twenty-five years. Our overall standard was nicely caught by a remark of Richard Usborne's. Richard was an advertising man, a best-selling social historian, and our only performer in a class comparable with the captain's. But his *Punch* contributions, if not by his wish, were far from frequent. On those, he barely scraped his place. 'I can see', he muttered in the dressing-room, looking round at the rest of us weekly regulars, 'that I'm just being played for my cricket'. A true word, at that.

None of this is to say that the regulars, though rabbits to a man, lacked a proper feeling for the game. We had been schooled in it. Literally if long ago. We were steeped in its lore and legend; in what the Englishman thinks of, arrogantly but unrepentantly, as its essential Englishness: in our case, an Englishness as English as *Punch* itself. We rejoiced in its leisurely, mysterious rites, so impossible to de-mystify for those lesser breeds without the Laws. (Once, luring an Illinois acquaintance to the Oval, I explained helpfully at one point: 'Now they're going for the runs'. If I'd been talking to a sightscreen it couldn't have looked blanker. 'What else?' he asked. And went off into some rubbish about the Chicago Red Sox.)

So it was all there, deep down. We felt cricket. We knew cricket. We honoured and revered it. We just couldn't be said to play it.

We played other games. Or had done. Some of us. The art editor, Russell Brockbank, had been an ice-hockey man, but out in the middle at The Hague I think he missed his skates. Certainly missed the first straight puck. Cartoonist David Langdon, a golfing man still, teed off impressively, skying leg stump with his back swing. I was more an athletics man, myself, and still have a small crested spoon somewhere, runner-up, junior high jump.

Unfortunately, the brand-new score book disappeared after the game. There was a theory that Bernard Hollowood had secretly burnt it and scattered the ashes on his head. But from memory I believe Hollowood and Usborne were recorded in a fine opening stand of 46. I forget how Usborne went. But honourably, and later got into two consecutive editions of the magazine. After them we were all tail. But boosted the total to 53 all the same.

The Hague thrashed us without loss. Plenty of time, before our night-sailing, to return their hospitality of the evening before, which had been long, liquid and lavish. I don't say ours wasn't the same. But the atmosphere was different. They were very jolly. We were less so. Our captain was particularly quiet, falling into private thoughts.

One doesn't want, of course, to make excuses. That wouldn't be cricket…but they are a sharp people, those Netherlanders…well accustomed to Schnapps…No, no. All I'm thinking is that when we took the field after lunch, earlier on the great day, our captain had said to theirs: 'I'm afraid one of my bowlers is drunk.' This drew the laughing reply: 'Still, or again?' Demonstrating a grasp of our national idiom equalling that of our national game. Let alone an eye for a tactical advantage.

The crossing back to Harwich was different too. We had come over in calm waters, brilliant sun, even high expectations. No sun going home. We spotted that, despite somewhat impaired faculties. It's what you have to accept after midnight. A full moon, but only glimpsed intermittently between racing clouds. The gale screamed. Yesterday's blue millpond was rising in hurtling green towers. The ship proceeded in corkscrew plunges. Left to me, we wouldn't have put to sea. But captains of ships, as of cricket, are undissuadable from such lunatic ventures.

Not saying a lot, we braced ourselves against the bar until it closed. And not much more even after Philip Hubbard, gifted versifier and twelfth man, found a way round the back and opened it again. Bernard, who left early for the cabin he was sharing with Hubbard, didn't say anything.

Ship's officers had strongly advised us to get in our bunks and stay there. Even when we took their advice, much, much later, neither process was easy. I was sharing with Brockbank. We pretended not to notice the long, shuddering gaps between body and bunk. We pretended to sleep. Which took courage. Which was Dutch, and we'd had plenty. But we were still well awake when Hubbard burst in on us with alarming news. Bernard Hollowood had never appeared in the cabin, was out loose, somewhere on the howling deck, whence all but he had fled.

Everyone but Usborne having retired fully-dressed, a search party was quickly on its way, made up of everyone else. Well, not me. I wasn't feeling well enough, as it happened, so I can only report subsequent events as reported to me. But I knew well, despite personal preoccupations, what forebodings filled the searchers. Could even share them. If our editor and captain had gone to his death, perhaps inviting the tempest to sweep him overboard to drown his grief and shame, this was horribly serious. A new editor? We could all be out of a job.

It didn't come to that, thank God. According to reports, not all agreeing in detail, as the rags of cloud tore clear of the moon, they found him. In a lifeboat, aft. Some said he held an empty glass, others that he wore his Staffordshire cap, its peak screwed round to about mid-off.

'Get out,' he croaked at the close field of pale faces. Everyone agreed on that. Hubbard claimed an impulse to say that this was just what we'd done, earlier in the day, but decided the time wasn't right. The editor was not for joking.

But I can tell you first-hand that those were the last two words we got out of him until the Monday staff conference, back in the office. And he didn't say a lot, even then. And never mentioned cricket at all.

Quite unusual, for him.

FANTASIA
IAN WALLACE

His career as an opera singer, actor and broadcaster has taken up far too much time in the summer months that would have been better spent at Lord's or anywhere else where a cricket match was in progress. Unfortunately it still does. His playing days began and ended in obscurity at school.

It was all right for Mike Denness. He had an athletic father who, no doubt, introduced him to short-pitched tennis balls that lifted and left him in some West of Scotland garden when he was five and a half. My father, also a Scot, was fifty-one and short-sighted when I was born and I don't think he ever played cricket in his life. That didn't prevent him going round Spey Bay golf course in the same number of strokes as his age when he was seventy-four.

His firm promoted him and sent him to London before I was born, but bowling at me on our mossy lawn was never suggested or attempted, and though my mother was twenty-one years his junior and a sneaky under-arm server at tennis, it never occurred to her to prepare me with leg-breaks or cleverly disguised googlies for summer afternoons at an English preparatory school in the late 1920s. Coming from Glasgow she just didn't have it in her.

When I went to my prep school in Hampstead I soon realized that all my peers had fathers who had given them a grasp of the essentials of the game before they'd ever set foot in the place. My father could only buy me a nice bat autographed by J.B. Hobbs, and my mother, always a one for keeping the furniture spotless, pitched in a bottle of linseed oil. I oiled the wretched willow pretty well every day. The house reeked of it.

Old Brigadier-General Stone, the prep school bursar, and the only man I've ever met who took mustard with fish, used to coach the more promising boys in a solitary net at the end of the playground where the pitch was a long coconut mat laid on the concrete. I watched him intently, his ancient joints creaking like a three-masted grain ship rounding Cape Horn, as he bowled off a three-pace run with what I now realize must have been an immaculate line and length. He never bowled at me. I wasn't promising. I didn't even know how to hold my aromatic, oozing bat.

It would be wickedly unfair to blame my parents' ignorance of cricket for the fact that I never played for England, Middlesex, Charterhouse, even for my house there – or indeed anything other than the lowliest team available to boys of my age at that excellent establishment on a hill above Godalming, which long after my departure nurtured and developed the talents of one P.B.H. May.

No, the reason why I could not, like Mike Denness, be a Scots captain of England or, like Peter May, manage it after five years on top of that Surrey hill, was very simple. They had a talent for cricket. I had not. Yet when it came to enthusiasm and keenness, kindled by watching the likes of T.R. Garnett or J.M. Lomas nearing a century on one of the most beautiful school cricket grounds in England during that magical hour on a Saturday morning between the end of lessons and lunch, the gap between me and the giants became a good deal narrower.

Yes, my unrequited love affair with cricket had begun but at Charterhouse I soon had to resort to what many lovers have been driven to throughout history when the object of their affection fails to respond. I began to indulge in fantasies. In the 1930s cricket was all but compulsory, like chapel and the Officers' Cadet Corps. I played for 'Second Tics,' the lowest team in the house. Its curious description had nothing to do with parasites or nervous twitches, it was a contraction of the word peripatetics. Each house fielded a collection of their under-16 duds which played two two-day matches every week against similar opposition from the other houses in a league of depressing mediocrity. Among the many classes of cricket played at the school this was definitely steerage. Our side usually included poor Tony Goulding Brown, a brilliant history scholar, who came in at number eleven, looked owlishly down the pitch through his thick glasses, and held his bat motionless until such time as the bowler managed to hit the stumps. In this class of cricket he often had to wait several overs. When eventually he heard the cheerful rattle behind him he muttered a word of thanks to the Almightly and resumed his seat and his book until called upon to stand rather than field at long-stop. He did not bowl. We all greatly respected him.

I referred to him as poor because despite his enormous intellect he died in his rooms at Trinity College, Cambridge a very few years later from a surfeit of study and lack of sleep or exercise, all sustained on a diet of little else than jam and chocolate biscuits.

But even in a team that could find room for such players as he, I was capable of transforming our matches, in my imagination, into Test matches at Lord's. Ignoring the five other games taking place on the same field, where someone else's boundary hit could hurtle across your square at right-angles to the ball you were facing, I was Wallace, unexpectedly called upon to open the English innings with Herbert Sutcliffe. On the rare occasions that I bowled my varied selection of long-hops, full-tosses and donkey-drops it was Wallace attacking Bradman or McCabe after an exhausted Larwood had had to be rested. It was harmless and wafted me happily through the afternoon. I think I was the only member of our team who was sorry when it was time to draw stumps. Incidentally, I had never been to Lord's or a Test match.

I regret to say, however, that one of those golden afternoons lives in my memory as the day that the gilt was summarily removed from the gingerbread, to say nothing of the smile of achievement from my chubby rubicund features. Our opposing team, even judged by the standards of this mediocre league, was somewhat short of strike bowlers, or indeed bowlers of any description. To compound their problems the wicket-keeper had forgotten to bring the gloves and our 'keeper was not in a generous mood. When we won the toss and decided to bat I doubt if Ladbroke's would have accepted any bets on the result. If ever there was a foregone conclusion we were it.

Our side went to work with aggression. The house captain – a revered member of the school 1st XI – had offered any member of the team who scored a hundred or took five wickets a tizzy (sixpenny) ice with syrup and cream from the tuckshop. A tizzy ice filled a half-pint tumbler with succulent pink ice cream the same colour as the 1st XI blazer. With strawberry syrup and a generous pouring of double cream it was our equivalent of ambrosial nectar.

Herbert Sutcliffe and I opened the batting against an extraordinarily weak Australian attack. He soon departed mistiming a short-pitched delivery that bounced twice before reaching him. I, on the other hand, was punishing the bad balls mercilessly. There were about half a dozen of them in every over. Suddenly our captain declared.

When we reached the long grass I asked the bespectacled youth who was scoring how many I had made. 'Ninety-nine not out,' he replied, without looking up. Our captain was horrorstruck, the rest of the team reduced to an awed silence. The two captains conferred, mention was made of the luscious tumblerful snatched from my grasp by this impulsive closure of the innings. It was decided that the declaration should be waived. We all trooped back to the wicket where I dispatched a charitable delivery far enough to run one. We declared again and subsequently won by an innings.

When I claimed my prize the house captain refused to pay up. 'You can't waive a declaration,' said he. Some loud-mouthed idiot had leaked the story so the captain knew what had happened before I got to him. 'Sorry, Wallace, ninety-nine not out was creditable but doesn't qualify.' I believe he went on to a distinguished career in the Sudan Civil Service. Unprotesting I walked forlornly to the tuck shop and bought

myself a Mars bar. That was only twopence.

Even such a disillusioning experience did not snuff out my affection for the game at which I was so bad and which I enjoyed playing so much, though I knew that that day was my playing zenith. Yet soon afterwards, during the summer exeat weekend, I discovered the joy of seeing the real thing. I paid my first visit to Lord's, squeezing in just before they closed the gates, and stood close-packed, peering from behind the grandstand opposite the Mound at Hedley Verity demolishing Australia on a sticky dog in those joyous days when covers were unknown. And if after the war my enthusiasm needed a shot in the arm it was amply provided, again at Lord's, by the sight of Denis Compton and Bill Edrich scampering cheeky singles and scoring elegant fours against South Africa. That booster has remained in my bloodstream ever since.

I also had a fantasy about watching cricket. It has become reality. Through the great good fortune of knowing a few cricketers, notably Alf Gover, I can now don my MCC tie and sit on a high stool in the Long Room or on the top tier of the pavilion behind the bowler's arm – a magnificent privilege – and spectate to my heart's content. When, occasionally, I see great players sucumbing to public displays of ill-temper it occurs to me that if at the age of fifteen they had been denied a tizzy ice – with syrup and cream – because rules are rules, they might be able to accept the swings as well as the roundabouts of the game a little more philosophically.

VAIN MEMORIES

JOHN FOWLES

The story of his development as a cricketer is told in his essay. In summary, he was captain of Bedford School 1st XI in 1944 and later played for New College, Oxford. For a short period he also played first-team cricket for Southend and for Newton Abbot.

I have not seriously touched ball or bat for over thirty years now, but there was a time when cricket took up a very large part of my life, both physically and imaginatively; and in a sense, the latter one, it still does. Something in me still sees novels – and not only my own – as cricket games: and their writing, as having to bowl against some fiendishly good batsmen (the readers) on a featherbed wicket. Cricket remains for me the game of games, the sanspareil, the great metaphor, the best marriage ever devised of mind and body. None of the other sports we British have given the world – neither soccer nor rugby, nor golf, nor tennis – can begin to touch it. For me it remains the Proust of pastimes, the subtlest and most poetic, the most past-and-present; whose beauty can lie equally in days, in a whole, or in one tiny phrase, a blinding split second.

In many ways I was by chance born into the pink in cricketing terms. My father had been quite a good amateur player in his youth before the 1914–18 War, and had seen or even played against, at club level, many of the greats of that period. He claimed to have been present on an occasion when W.G. Grace, having hit a skier towards a safe pair of hands in the deep outfield, bellowed 'Innings declared!'; and with a glare at the umpires and an imperious beckon to his partner, started marching off before the ball was even caught. (He was on the only not-out score in the 90s he had never previously recorded.) I'm sure the story is apocryphal, but then so are most cricket stories, like all novels. I am without any records or *Wisden,* and wouldn't guarantee any I tell here.

My father's ideal had been Ranji, with a soft spot also for Trumper, among the batsmen. In the present of my childhood it was Frank Woolley. When he came with Kent to play our county side it was always a red-letter day, especially when the celebrated leg glance was on display. We went to all the local Essex matches, only a few hundred yards from where we lived, Chalkwell Park at Leigh-on-sea, or at Victoria Park in Southend nearby. I suppose as a small boy I saw almost all the great players of the 1930s on those two grounds. 'Patsy' Hendren, Verity (the great enigma, how could he bowl such dollies, yet reduce 'our' men to such painful, prodding anxiety?), Larwood (especially terrifying on that small Chalkwell Park ground, I seem to recall one bumper of his that went clean over the keeper's head and over the boundary in two enormous bounces), Hammond (a drive that towered over the tall trees on the Leigh Road side, and still the most majestic straight six I have ever seen struck); many others.

This was far from all. The headmaster of my prep-school, just beyond the Chalkwell ground, was Denis Wilcox, then captain of the county side, and coach of the school side; and who combined the two in terms of the distinguished other cricketers he would coax to our nets (and coax cherished autographs from, also). By the age of thirteen I had been given a batting point or two by Hendren and even 'faced' the formidable Essex fast bowler, Kenneth Farnes. He would only take one lazy step to the wicket to deliver very gently against us small boys; but he would also usually bowl a few at full run-up and speed to the empty net. I rather suspect that these fearsome demonstrations of reality put more of us off cricket than the reverse.

Then, when I was first allowed to cycle to school, I was put under the wing of an older day-boy, who lived a few doors up from us in our own road. He was already the hero of the school, dazzling at both cricket and soccer, the one person we all dreamt of being. His name was Trevor Bailey. Later in life I had to face him in a match between our two public schools, Bedford and Dulwich. I managed to keep him out of my wicket, but I suspect that was more out of Trevor's kindness, and the memory of many daily journeys together, than through my skill.

I was a bat until I was fourteen or fifteen, but then (through my own foolishness) permanently damaged my eyesight by surreptitiously reading through an attack of scarlet fever. Bedford School had two excellent coaches at that time: a young master and recent Cambridge University fast bowler, Jack Webster, and an old pro, Ben Bellamy. Ben had been the Northamptonshire wicket-keeper, and still kept very sharply in practice games, coaching both batsmen between balls, and the bowlers between overs. They turned me into what was then known as a 'swerve' bowler. In the end, when I had quelled every schoolboy's dream and learnt the seamer's art has little to do with sheer speed, I could manage both swings and their respective cutters, although God knows I never mastered them. It always seemed hazard much more than anything else that produced the killing balls. My fortes were said to be 'late swerve' and 'nip off the wicket', but I never had the least idea what produced them. I'm sorry 'swerve' has dropped from cricketing vocabulary: that sudden, almost magical deviation half-way down the trajectory...they call it 'late swing' now, but 'swerve' still expresses it better, to my mind.

I got into the Bedford first eleven when I was sixteen, and captained it in my last year at school. Much was made of my getting several former Test players' wickets during that last season. I can't remember them all now; one was 'Gubby' Allen's (he played against us every year, still uncomfortably quick for our batsmen), and I had the old England captain, R.E.S. Wyatt, twice. But the most memorable came in a charity match, with Learie Constantine (then in Lancashire League) as the star of the opposition. A considerable audience turned up to watch him; no one else mattered. He had had a difficult and tiring journey to the ground, and it was tacitly agreed we should give him a few easy deliveries to get his eye in. I was bowling when he appeared, and duly delivered a short and wide outswinger, well off the stumps, for him to practise on. The great man shaped up to administer the savage square cut the ball deserved; fatally changed his mind, dabbed at it – and straight to the best fielder we had in our team, who was at gully. There was a horrified silence all round the ground, not a single clap. It was like one of the old Bateman cartoons: the Man Who Dared To... When we came off, the headmaster told me what was already only too apparent: that I was now the most hated young man in Bedfordshire. He condemned me to 'buying Mr Constantine all the Guinness he chooses to drink', while waiting for his train after the match. In fact I had an hour alone with him afterwards, of far more value to me in human terms than cricket ones. I had some of the thoughtless colour prejudice ubiquitous in public schoolboys in those days; it had been comprehensively destroyed by the end of that hour. I have always supported the West Indies teams since then, even against England.

I was to have such a scalp only once more in my life, playing for New College at Oxford against E.W. Swanton's XI. 'Jim' announced beforehand, not without a hint of warning, that he was bringing a 'useful' sailor, then I think a sickberth killick (leading seaman). When the young man duly turned up in his uniform, we were sceptical. When he came to the wicket, I was fielding at mid-off, and I remember seeing him lean gently towards a seemingly good-length ball, clearly not a serious offensive stroke. Almost simultaneously the ball was going through my legs, without my even getting a touch to it. That, and other strokes, soon ended our complacency. I came on to bowl against him myself, and suffered heavily. I knew the only ball that might have him, an inswinger on the leg stump that cut back and took the off, but I could not produce it; anything even faintly off line or length was sent like a bullet to the boundary, and with a maddening ease and lack of effort. This was not a sailor chancing his arm;

but a lethal genius, far more killer than killick.

I've never understood why some batsmen have this supreme, almost supernatural sense of timing; many great ones at the highest level, and great scorers also, lack it. Colin Cowdrey had it; so does Gower, at his best. And so did this modest young man from the Navy, better known now as P.B.H. May. I did get him in the expensive end, with the kind of ball I have mentioned. But my pleasure was somewhat dimmed by Swanton himself, who was batting at the other end. 'Wonder you didn't bowl that one overs ago,' was his dry comment, as May departed. Ah well. At least he was supposing in me a gift that I didn't have.

The conflict with another side of my nature first became clear at Oxford. I had no notion then I would become a writer, but I was already a keen naturalist and interested in the arts. I was offered University trials, but failed to turn up for them; already I began to sense that 'adult', quasi-professional cricket was not for me. I lacked the true skill, and even more, the true concentration. Bowling the very occasional 'unplayable' ball is one thing; producing it regularly is very much something else. I still played during vacations for the Southend town club in Essex, which was of high standard, with several players hovering on the county fringes, and also for Newton Abbot in Devon, whose cricket was of lower standard, but much more fun. Most fun of all was a casual New College cricket team made up of 'good' players and enthusiastic rabbits. We had a tie emblazoned with a duck, with as many eggs below as the member had merited. A tour of the Tavistock area in Devon we did about 1948 was a revelation. Village cricket was remote from the sort I had been playing till then, and its enjoyability, *not* taking the game very seriously, was delicious.

Perhaps delicious was not always the word. One match we played, against a tiny village on the fringes of Dartmoor, was the very opposite. It was on a steeply sloping field, only too evidently normally used as cow pasture. The pitch was rough beyond belief; and to top everything (as we had been warned) the village *had a bowler*. I can't remember if he was what he should have been by tradition, the local blacksmith. But he was decidedly quick, by village standards; and on that pitch, totally unplayable. Conversation among those of us nervously waiting to go in was very rapidly confined to one topic only: how to survive, not in cricket terms, but purely physical ones – in other words, how best to get out as soon as possible. I have seen the great West Indian bowlers in full flood; but still rate that match as the single most frightening cricket experience I ever personally had.

By the age of 25 I had given up playing cricket for ever; the completeness with which I did this was as it is with some drug cures. Withdrawal has to be total, if it is to succeed. But total withdrawal from cricket is impossible. Now, if only vicariously, through television, I become duly addicted again each summer. Friends think I remain disgustingly aloof from the living game. I don't go to Test or county matches, or to those of our local club here in Dorset (whose capital in cricket terms is Taunton); I've never had anything to do with the various publishers' and authors' teams. This is true. I remain aloof from the game in many ways; but emphatically not at heart.

Medieval theologians used to dispute how the angels in heaven spent their time, when not balancing on needle points and singing anthems to the Lord. I know. They slump glued to their clouds, glasses at the ready, as the Archangel Michael (that well-known slasher) and stonewalling St Peter open against the Devil's XI. It could not be Heaven, otherwise.

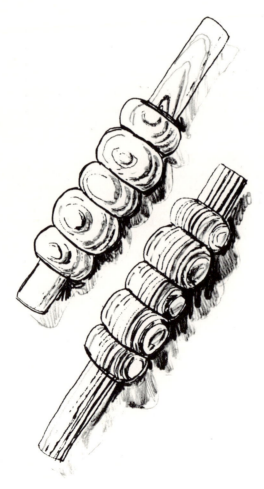

GEOGRAPHICAL CRICKET
JEREMY KEMP

Introduced to the game by an elder sister skilled at hoicks over midwicket; fetching and carrying for her turned him at an early age into a wicket-keeper. A great admirer of Lindwall among the 1948 Australians, he also readily identified with Tallon whose role seemed to offer the richest possible blend of paradise and purgatory. Has 'stood' many times for the Lord's Taverners, contributing to such immortal scorelines as 'c Kemp b Trueman', 'c Kemp b Snow', 'c Kemp b Rumsey' and, more obscurely, 'c Kemp b Frindall'.

'An unholy row over a roller,' the headline read, 'team's hopes flattened before match begins.' This almost totally incomprehensible piece of journalism set me off thinking about the potential influence of the Almighty upon the course of coarse cricket – or the more refined version for that matter.

Who can ever be sure for example, that the name Thomas Lord is wholly coincidental? After all, we are told that the deity moves in mysterious ways to bring about his wonders. Maybe He looks down upon the headquarters in much the same way as Father Time, but unseen of course, and not least during the 1985 final between the village adversaries from Fifeshire and Surrey. However, such influence as He may conjure up must be fragile rather than absolute, otherwise one would confidently expect such a final to take place between, say, Barnwell All Saints and Chilton Trinity...or at the very least Gussage Saint Michael and Morley Saint Botolph.

Quite where Saint Botolph ranks in the hagiography of the Church of England I do not know. What I do know is that the sainthood is remarkably well represented in the shires. This wide representation includes such unlikely chaps as Saint Arvans, Saint Blazey, Saint Budeaux,

123

Saint Clement (nominally in charge of the weather?). But happily no Saint Swithin. Then there is Saint Endellion, Saint Dogwells and Saint Ewe, and Saint Judas (not to be trusted in a limited over contest – 'Count the men in the inner ring, skipper'). There is also Saint Minver and Saint Pancras, strictly a touring side. To round off the selection there is Saint Petrox and Saint Quivox. Who knows, some of them might even be 'Holy Romans'? Does the Vatican, do you think, have an official attitude towards cricket? Italy, surprisingly, has a national side... Are Catholic teams permitted to play Sunday fixtures or to refresh themselves on the Sabbath? The latter restriction might more readily apply to Saint Illtyd or Saint Asaph who would, as good non-conformists, turn out to be *bona fide* travellers to a man.

Place names exert an influence that, while it may be fragile, has undoubted potential. Who would dare to adjudicate in a contest between Batts Corner and Barton le Willows? Would one suggest that either started with an unfair advantage, or simply conclude that the latter supplied the former and leave it at that? What might one say about Mid Cowbog (Banffshire) versus Muckfoot (Ayrshire)? Bring on the Scottish heavy roller and flatten their Celtic hopes? Imagine the billing at Lords of Catbrain versus Mousehole. Cow Honeybourne versus Donkey Town. Dog village versus Cat and Fiddle Inn (good scrap this one). You could legitimately stage the Welsh area final between Farmyard (Clwyd) and Farmers (Dyfed), given a little help from above and doubtless plenty of 'cowshots' on display.

To develop the theme, but not to do it too brown, there are a few additional categories I would like to mention. It is a fairly childish game and anyone with an extensive knowledge of the British Isles could certainly play it. The department of mischief could follow with Dangerous Corner versus Crossroads, Crazies Hill versus Cripplestyle, Dragons Green versus Druid, Fence versus Law, Gallows Green versus Hanging Langford, and finally once again close to the heart of the Almighty...Hassocks versus Kneesall, or maybe Nether Cassock...

Another short section bearing obvious significance would include Heath versus Wilson (out of date a little), Hutton versus Washbrook (never out of date) and Moscow versus Washington (County Durham)...alas only too constantly topical. The final section in this imaginary 'geographical cricket' inevitably involves the mildly risqué, but I do not believe that any of these fairly innocent combinations would encourage the censor to twitch and reach for his red, or blue, pencil. However, journalists would surely be drawn towards any of the following fixtures. Sponsors too would queue up for the opportunity to support Rake versus Maidenhead, Buttocks Booth versus Pratts Bottom, Flushing versus Looe, Meikle Tarty versus White Ladies Aston, and quite vulgarly Peover Superior versus North Piddle. What advice might a skipper give to his 'keeper when opposed to Barton in

the Beans or similarly Thornton le Beans????

There are many more tempting fixtures which would include the Roman ones like Aston Juxta Mondrum versus Toller Porcorum. Lover versus Blissgate, Filby versus Burgess Hill. In order that Mr Tony Lewis can be certain of finding the occasional commentating job I finish up with DWYGYFYLCHI versus CEFN COED Y CYMMER.

Someone frightfully wise, whose name I cannot recall, developed a theory about God as an ironist, and if an ironist why not a humourist. One certainly needs a highly developed sense of humour to cope with some of the things He gets up to, not least on the cricket field.

'Team's hopes flattened before match begins,' was my starting point. I am now approaching my concluding one. Despite a very proper build-up, and much speculation upon the outcome, many cricket matches (Saint Clement and Saint Swithin) sadly do not even begin. Thus I conclude with another headline which clearly demonstrates the Almighty in His role of ironist or humourist, and emphatically confirms his influence over the course of coarse cricket. It read: 'Match cancelled due to good weather...Harvest seen as clear priority.'

CRICKET SAVES THE DAY
SIR ELDON GRIFFITHS

Captained his grammar school XI and played college cricket at Cambridge before leaving the game to work overseas as a journalist in non-cricketing parts. His farewell gift from his friends in New York was a cricket match between the editors (male) and the researchers (female) of Newsweek. Later played for Crawley and is a non-playing and, to his regret, generally absentee Taverner.

One of the myths of contemporary politics is that sport improves international relations. My experience as Minister of Sport was very different. True, the so-called bamboo curtain was penetrated for the first time when British and Chinese ping pong teams started playing against one another; but the Olympic Games in Munich produced a massacre of Israeli athletes by Palestinian terrorists and since then scores of international football matches have led to riots, bad blood and the tragedy in Brussels when Liverpool's football hooligans ran amuck and people were killed.

Nor is cricket immune to international punch-ups, as anyone who has toured India, Pakistan or even the West Indies can testify. The burning issue of playing Test matches against the South Africans likewise continues to excite political passions, and even violence, in all corners of the Commonwealth.

Cricket nonetheless remains a source of friendship and mutual respect among the cricketing nations. And on one memorable occasion an eccentric cricket match did as much as anything else to put a stop to a squabble between Britain and the United States.

The two countries had collided head on over Sir Anthony Eden's decision to re-open the Suez Canal by force after the Egyptian dictator, Gamal Abdel Nasser, seized it in 1956. President Eisenhower's reaction was to threaten financial sanctions and, under American pressure, the British and French withdrew from Suez amid angry recriminations. The Anglo-American community in England split wide open over

127

Washington's harsh treatment of its closest ally. Life-long friends quarrelled fiercely. Americans and their best friends in London stopped talking to one another.

At the time I was Chief European Correspondent for *Newsweek* magazine. I was summoned to a series of meetings with British Ministers and senior backbenchers at the House of Commons who were seeking to heal the rift between Washington and Westminster. With a number of friends from the US press corps, Anglo-American banks, traders and film people, we decided that one of the best ways of composing these differences was through the two countries' shared interest in sport – and good humour. Hence the decision to stage a Trans-Atlantic cricket match. It would be played on the next anniversary of the British Army's burning down the White House in 1812, with the prize – in place of the ashes – being a box of those tea leaves whose dumping in the sea off Boston brewed up the American revolution.

The Lord's Taverners promptly accepted our invitation to represent Britain at this match. The United States team, aptly named the American Amateurs, was to be made up of US ex-patriates in London, supported as necessary by a 'borrowed' fast bowler and one county class batsman, in recognition of the fact that the British used 'mercenaries' when they sacked Washington (and, in any event, the Amateurs would hardly stand a chance without at least one decent bowler and batsman). The Royal Artillery volunteered its splendid sports ground at Woolwich as the venue for our match. The United States Third Air Force agreed to provide its 120-strong marching band to lead the entertainment.

Volunteers for places in the American Eleven were soon queueing up in droves. The match caught the imagination of the entire Anglo-American community to the point where a prominent US banker complained that it wasn't cricket that the London representative of his main competitor had secured a place on the team, while his own man in London had been left out. Pan American and TWA also vied for places, the former winning the battle (and a place for its London PR man, Fred Tupper, in the team) with an irresistible offer to fly our Boston tea leaves across the Atlantic for nothing.

Within days, the American Amateurs, led by Yale Newman, the diminutive London correspondent of ABC Television, were fitting themselves out with flannels and cricket boots; devouring every book on cricket they could lay their hands on; crowding into the nets at Westminster School and Lord's to try their hand at a totally unfamiliar game. To assist the Americans, *Time* magazine published a primer on how to play cricket, parts of which read as follows:

'Some people think that cricket is a kind of grasshopper. Cricket does involve hopping on the well-kept grass of Lord's or other cricket grounds, but only in a sedate and profoundly ordered way. The sport of cricket and its curiously languid vocabulary (Samples: "Well-played, sir", for "Great catch", and "Howzat?" for "Is he out?") are as British as a crumpet. Some believe they represent the unifying forces that bind the Empire together.

'No one knows how cricket began. When the Spanish Armada sailed in 1588, shepherds in South England were already playing the game in their sheep pens. Today the dullish clunck of cricket bats sounds in 29 countries, and the annual Test Matches between England and Australia have become a sort of World Series, with a difference.

'Watching cricket is easy. All anyone needs is a deckchair, a pipe or knitting, and a week off from the office. Playing is more onerous since it requires white flannels, spiked shoes, wickets, a bat and a leather-covered ball. There are two wickets, situated at opposite ends of the cricket pitch (never field), and they are quite important. Each consists of three stumps of wood driven into the turf, with two bails, small bits of wood shaped like spark plugs, balanced on top. From one wicket, 66 feet away, the bowler (never pitcher) tries to knock the bails off the other wicket. The batsman (never batter) attempts to thwart the bowler and, possibly, to hit the ball past the fielders and over the boundary (never wall). Runs are scored by trotting between the two wickets.

'Most bowlers bounce the ball, relying on spin and irregularities in the turf to fool the batsman. The surest defence is to hold the bat so that the broad blade rests directly in front of the wicket. This reduces the bowler's target to a hairbreadth and is called stone walling...a tactic that is not popular with onlookers.

'There are no foul lines in cricket, and the ball may be batted either forward or backward, factors that put fielders to severe tests. For reasons that elude researchers, a fielder close to the batter's left is called "silly mid-on". Presumably for the same reason, the man a few feet off to the right is called "silly mid-off".

'The big league batsman's record is 452. A few years ago Jim Laker of England set a significant mark among bowlers when he skittled (never struck) out nineteen Australians in two innings during the Fourth Test Match. The London press cried that he had "Lakered" the Aussies, enlarging cricket's odd vocabulary.'

The day of the match dawned clear and sunny. As captain of the American Amateurs, I led onto the Woolwich pitch a motley team of US broadcasters, journalists, bankers, businessmen and diplomats. Several of them wore American football helmets. One had a large L-plate on his shirt. The Lord's Taverners were skippered by Leo Bennett, former captain of Northamptonshire, who had just completed building the BBC's new TV centre at Lime Grove. His team included Stuart Surridge, Ben Barnett and half a dozen stage and TV personalities, prominent among them the inimitable Dickie Hearn, alias Mr Pastry, wearing his chef's apron and

Chaplinesque bowler hat.

Lord Tedder, former Chief of Staff of the RAF, tossed the coin – and the Amateurs chose to bat first. The BBC's John Snagge was an umpire.

Neither of the American openers had ever taken guard before. The only kind of ball they had ever hit with a bat was a full toss, hurled at chest level by a baseball pitcher. Taking pity on his crossbatted opponent, the Taverner's opening bowler tossed half a dozen short balls outside the American's leg stump. The first wicket promptly fell to a splendid catch at deep square leg; the second Amercian was stumped when he swung and missed by a mile; a third fell flat on his face, six feet outside the crease.

It was the fall of these early wickets that led the Taverners to make a fatal mistake. Convinced that the Americans would be all out within the first few overs, Leo Bennett sportingly told his bowlers to serve up full tosses. The Amateurs response was to thump every other delivery over the boundary for sixes. There were Yankee cheers from the pavilion when 100 went up with the loss of only five wickets at the end of 80 minutes. The Taverners then reverted to medium-paced bowling on the off-stump. Three Americans were caught in the slips, one more was quickly run out. I then sent in my secret weapon, a Somerset county player who qualified for the Amateurs by virtue of his having been born of British parents while visiting the Middle West. This man merrily proceeded to carve up the Taverners' bowling, scoring all round the wicket at a pace that put on a further 90 runs, while I grimly stonewalled at the other end. Our partnership, to which this Yank from Somerset contributed all but three or four runs, brought the Americans' score at tea-time to a useful 196 for 9. The Amateurs then declared.

After tea, Stuart Surridge and Ben Barnett opened for the Taverners. They took the score to 30 or 40 without loss, then switched to batting left-handed. Surridge was promptly caught by an American wearing a baseball mitt on the long-on boundary. Taking pity on the Amateurs' bowling, which at that stage consisted mainly of awkwardly tossed lobs, most of which fell a yard or more outside the wicket, Barnett and the next three Taverners concentrated on giving the fielders some badly needed catching practice. Five wickets fell smartly before Mr Pastry came in. He soon had the crowd in stitches with his antics.

The Taverners' score nevertheless went on rising; I therefore brought out my second secret weapon. He was a Cambridge University bowler of near Test match quality who had acquired a US passport when his parents emigrated to New York. And his first delivery removed the middle stump of the Taverners' best-known batsman. The whole balance of the match thereby altered in favour of the Americans. Leo Bennett, who was now at the wicket, thereupon told the remaining Taverners batsmen to abandon the niceties and put their backs into winning the match. That was the signal for the band of the United States Third Air Force to enter the lists. Trumpets and trombones blaring, all 120 bandsmen, preceded by an enormous drum major, invaded the pitch, playing *Hold that Tiger.* And, knowing nothing of the rules of cricket, the band took it for granted that they were allowed to march up and down, so long as they stayed behind the wicket – behind the mound, as one of them put it.

'Clear off,' shouted the Taverners. They might as well have been addressing the Niagara Falls. Cymbals clashing, drums booming, the Third Air Force continued to parade up and down the field behind the stumps at the bowler's end, completely disconcerting the remaining batsmen. The umpires could, of course, have ordered the game to be halted until these intruders were removed; but John Snagge and the Taverners' captain sportingly refused to interfere – and the crowd, quite obviously, loved it.

Leo Bennett's team paid the price for his sportsmanship. Their concentration fell away; the scoring rate dropped; three more wickets fell in quick succession. By 6.30 pm the Taverners were all out. The Amateurs had won by 16 runs!

To cheers from the pavilion, Lord Tedder presented a silver cup, filled with the Boston tea leaves, to the Americans' astonished captain. Both teams then repaired, arm in arm, to the Officers' Mess. That night, amid the silver plate of the Royal Artillery, the wine flowed freely, the conversation was animated, the laughter was long and loud. Thanks to cricket the Americans and the British were back together again. The traumas of Suez were forgotten.

AFTERWORD
OF AN AVERAGE FAN
MICHAEL LEITCH

Born in Middlesex. First glimpse of first-class cricket: arriving at Lord's after play had begun, hearing a great roar and rushing to peer between the decks at the Nursery End, just in time to see Denis Compton hare past and complete a splendid running catch on the long-leg boundary. Whew! Later captained Dulwich College Preparatory School 1st XI in 1953, from which summer his best playing memories are derived. Scheduled to make a comeback in 1986.

Nineteen eighty-five was a good year for reflecting about the game of cricket. The wettest summer anyone cares to remember was, fittingly, the year in which these 'Quick Singles' were written and collected. It was also, by coincidence, the year in which the book's house editor and a group of friends decided to make a series of organized break-outs from the village-in-a-minor-county where they live, and go to see some big-time matches. Here is his account of one oddly memorable day.

A Wednesday in early August, 1985. Assembly began at eight-thirty sharp in the Lounge Bar and shortly after nine, our breakfasts still blinking from an early shower of Morland's, we said goodbye to Margaret and stepped outside to look at the bus.

     An unexpectedly smart vehicle it turned out to be, almost new and more impressive by far than the one we'd had for Bath, its twelve plump seats covered in immaculate grey tweed, several shades paler than the damp clouds now piling up overhead.

     Still. Never mind the weather, the long-awaited day has come so let's get the picnic packed and off we go to Bristol to see Glocs v Notts in the quarter-final of the NatWest.

     At the wheel was Bob, also known as The Driver, who had nobly agreed to limit himself for the duration to occasional shandies. The other window seat in front was occupied by Andy, who as our navigator had with him a dog-eared road atlas of pre-motorway vintage, and behind him sat Bob, also known as The Landlord and now puffing on an eleven-inch cigar, Philip (very knowledgeable on pigeon racing), myself, Dave, and Jack who had never been to a cricket match before. Seven travellers in all, upliftingly freed for one day from the burdens of the building trade, estate management, road haulage, carmaking, licensed victualling, the selling of power tools, the editing of books…

Light rain spattered on the windows as we swung on to the A34 to Newbury and the M4, and the conversation turned to cricket. It was bound to be a good day, of course, they were two well-matched sides in good form, but would it go Gloucester's way, as we hoped? Best of all, might Lawrence tear 'em up? For those of us who like their cricket touched, *à la Hotspur,* with magical feats – lightning deliveries, splintering stumps, crushing analyses – he seemed the most likely matchwinner in the home side. All the same, in this year of their resurgence Gloucestershire had been well served by several less eye-catching cricketers, as we knew from our day at Bath. There, against the Somerset of Botham, Garner, Richards & Co, Gloucestershire had struggled back from 13 for three to top 300 by the close, thanks to resolute defence and shrewd hitting by Davison, Curran and Lloyds. Lawrence too had swished a bold six into the trees next to the pavilion, causing a West Indian spectator to urge him: 'Hit anudda six li' dat an' you getta *sponsah*!' Whereupon Lawrence was out. Finally, to send us home happy, Courtney Walsh had brought his howitzer to bear on those same trees, his score leaping from nought to thirty-plus in seven balls. With a team of such varied strengths, and before a home crowd, surely we Oxfordshire exiles would that evening bathe in the reflected glory of a win by our famous neighbour.

Notts, on the other hand, were Notts. A team of hard men, raised in the grit factories of both hemispheres: Rice, Hadlee, Robinson – now the name on everyone's lips after his feats against India and Australia – plus Broad, Hemmings and Mr Itching Powder himself, the great and unpredictable Derek Randall. Undoubtedly, we were in for a good day.

The rain grew steadily heavier the further west we drove, our route taking us through a chain of minor counties from our own Oxon into Berks and so to Wilts, where at least Gloucester now play one Sunday League match in the year, at Swindon. Despite the dark horizons, spirits were high among the touring party and various ritual jokes were aired. These involved, to take a random sample, The Driver's putative hairpiece ('Even if everybody else farted he wouldn't dare open the window') and the irrational fears of Dave once the cooling towers of Didcot were no longer in view ('They've gone, Dave, you can't see them anymore.' 'He's never been this far before, look at his little eyes going all over the place.' Guffaws.

'What you going to do on your holidays, Dave? Do they put a blindfold on you?' More guffaws, followed by Dave's cheerful comeback: 'I'll be all right on my holidays...because I won't have any of *you* buggers there.')

After a lightning provisions stop at the Carrefour supermarket near Swindon, which would have been even more lightning if half the bus hadn't got out and started queueing for bacon rolls, we resumed our westward journey through the spray and murk of a typical August morning. So typical, in fact, that the chances of a prompt ten-thirty start in Bristol were almost nil, and as the clock approached that hour we responded warmly to Andy's brilliant suggestion.

'Let's go to the Compass Inn,' said The Navigator. 'We can have one in there and phone the ground to see what's going on.'

Excellent. A spell indoors at Tormarton, away from the sodden countryside, would do us all some good, and a quarter of an hour later we were snug in the foyer bar with Bristol just a dozen miles away down the next hill. The phone call to Glocs CCC revealed that there had been no play and the next pitch inspection would be at twelve-thirty. Jack, the only man to start the day wearing a tie, removed it, rolled it neatly and placed it in the top pocket of his shirt. Another round was bought.

We were warm and comfortable in the Compass Inn but around 11.45 it stopped raining and we drove down to Bristol. After a lively difference over where to turn off between The Driver (an Exit 2 man) and The Navigator ('Exit 3, you prawn!') we somehow locked on to the yellow 'County Cricket' signs which nearly took us all the way. Bristol is not an easy place to find your way about, and the county ground keeps a surprisingly low profile behind a cluster of council buildings in a hilly and careworn suburb. It had seemed more picturesque on television. Ah well, here we were, and even though we immediately found that the pitch inspection had been postponed until one-thirty, no rain was actually falling as men in white coats ushered us to a distant car park. We unloaded, and soon were lugging our picnic boxes back across the main forecourt, when an official stopped us.

'I wouldn't go in there,' he said, nodding towards the entrance to the ground.

'Why not?' we said, 'we've only come ninety miles so far.'

'So you may,' he said, 'and there's nothing to stop you going in if you want to. But it's four quid each and in this weather...'

His voice trailed off. He might have added that there was next to no cover for ordinary spectators. Even so, had it been left to me, your correspondent, I would still have gone in, perhaps foolishly believing that the extra weight of our presence would be enough to flush the umpires and get some action started; but that was not the majority view. So, back we went to the bus, reloaded the picnic boxes and stepped round the corner to the nearest pub. Well, not the nearest, that was already filled with vexed cricket punters lining three deep at the bar. On to The Foresters, where our party nabbed the corner by the piano and settled down to wait until one-thirty. By then it was raining hard again.

We stuck to our task, and round followed round until we could all speak the familiar lines: 'That's three pints of bitter, a small shandy, a gin and tonic (ice *and* lemon, please), a Pils, and a Scotch with lots of water.' In the next hour the rain stopped, started again, it poured down, stopped, the sun came out, went in, more rain, then no rain, sun, rain... Every so often, dripping-wet figures entered the bar, shook their heads like dogs and gave out the latest news. Suddenly, a rumour went round the pub: the umpires had been out during one of the dry spells, then the Gloucestershire team had taken the field. Yes, it was true. Two lads near us had seen it. The fielders went to their positions, then the Notts openers came out of the pavilion and everyone cheered, the rain came slashing down, the umpires grabbed the bails and they all ran for it.

As the minutes ticked fruitlessly by, we wondered what to do. How about a dash to Taunton, where Somerset were playing Hampshire and they'd had a fairly normal morning's play? A kindly local said it would take about forty-five minutes on the motorway – plus another forty-five getting out of Bristol. We went off the idea. A place called Dirty Dursley was mentioned, said to have a strip club. No takers. Then Andy countered with his second brilliant suggestion.

'I think we should go and look at the SS *Great Britain*,' he said. Everyone agreed. Bob the Driver dashed through the latest downpour to retrieve the bus and drove us down to the docks. In the SS *GB* car park we lunched magnificently on a picnic provided by Bob (surely the day's hero) and slurped through a mound of water melon slices which Jack had brought. It was raining harder than ever but the sky was bright, and someone said: 'If this goes off by quarter to three we should go back to the cricket.' Agreed. It didn't. It went off at ten to three, but by then we were committed to going over the ship. In warm sunshine – the first of the day – we strode the decks and nosed about below, admiring the bulk and majesty of Brunel's superb creation, the first screw-propelled ship to cross the Atlantic, and the astonishing patient work of her restorers. Right, a quick dash round the gift shop and back to the cricket ground. If Gloucestershire were fielding, Lawrence would be bowling and that was something we all wanted to see. 'They'll probably go on till about eight,' said Dave. That was all right by us.

Our bus swept in at the car park entrance, all heads craning for a first glimpse of men in whites and a sight of the scoreboard. Funny... The field was empty and the car park deserted. Beyond the unmanned entrance, a thin scattering of people wandered around, outnumbered by gulls. Next to the blue vans of the BBC some technicians were winding up lengths of cable. An hour ago, we heard at last from a bystander, play had been abandoned for the day. A huddle of West Countrymen, gathered over a cider barrel outside the Jessop Tavern, gave us their version of the day's sporting highlight – the appearance on the edge of the pitch of the Nottinghamshire openers.

There can be few more desolate places than an abandoned cricket field. In twos and threes, moderately dumbstruck, we circled the ground and trod the outfield. Spongy. Over by the pavilion a tall West Indian carrying a cricket bag came through a door and walked past us. Must be Walsh, Lawrence looks younger, doesn't he? Even in that secret world beyond the folds of the hospitality tents, it was chucking-out time. At the entrance to the largest tent, an agitated caterer in a dark suit snapped the button on his walkie-talkie and held it to his mouth. 'Just clear the place,' he shouted to an invisible junior. 'Now!'

Many hours later, when the moon was thereabouts, I found the keyhole and stepped indoors and handed over my presents, an eraser stamped 'SS GREAT BRITAIN' and a pen, similarly marked. Then I

withdrew to the kitchen and began shaking my head and spluttering with almost hysterical laughter as the preposterousness of the whole day suddenly became clear. To my wife I said:

'How can seven grown men hire a bus, drive two hundred miles to watch a cricket match, come home after not a ball was bowled...and start planning another trip to see the same team when they come to Moreton-in-Marsh?'

She smiled at me in a kindly way. 'Well,' she said, 'it can't be because of the cricket, if there wasn't any.'

'No,' I said, agreeing. And yet, cricket was responsible for everything that had happened. We had spent the whole day in *an atmosphere of cricket*. Pubs also, it has to be said; but cricket first.

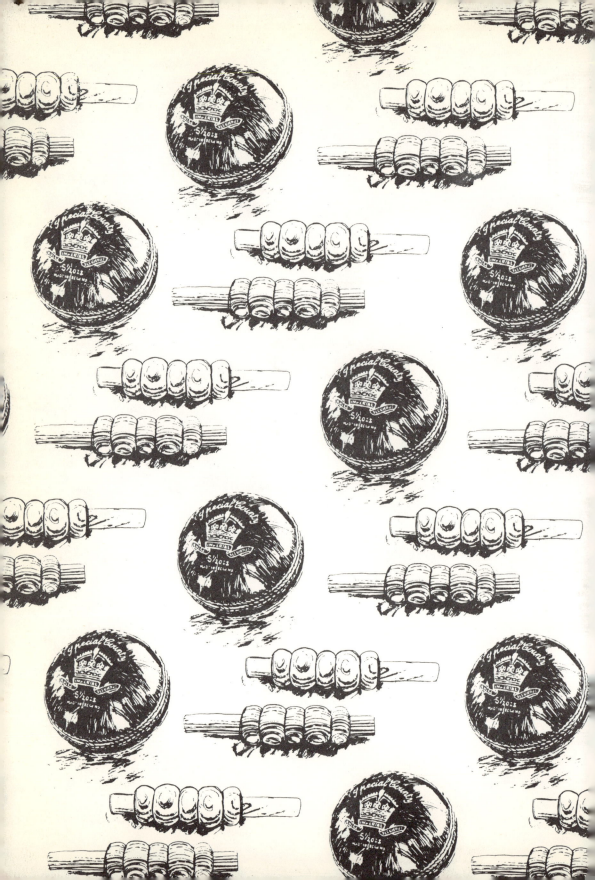